Changing Values:
How to Find Moral Truth in Modern Times

Changing Values:
How to Find Moral Truth in Modern Times

David Attwood

paternoster press

First published 1998 by Paternoster Press

04   03   02   01   00   99   98   7   6   5   4   3   2   1

Paternoster Press is an imprint of Paternoster Publishing,
P.O. Box 300, Carlisle, Cumbria CA3 0QS

British Library Cataloguing in Publication Data

A catalogue record for this book is available from the British Library.

ISBN 0-85364-806-9

This book is printed using Suffolk New Book paper which is 100% acid free

Typeset by WestKey Ltd, Falmouth, Cornwall
Printed in Great Britain by Clays Ltd, Bungay, Suffolk

Contents

Preface   vii

Introduction   1

1   Everyday Morality: Values   7
2   Simplicity and Complexity   22
3   Christian Love, the Foundation for Christian Ethics   32
4   Love, Rules and Truth-Telling   46
5   The Importance of Creation   60
6   Creation and Covenant   72
7   Creation and Sexuality   88
8   Covenant, Creation and Moral Rules   100
9   Euthanasia   113
10 The Demand for Perfection   129
11 Forgiveness and Moral Rigour   143
12 The Bible and Christian Ethics   155
13 The Authority of Conscience?   170
14 Christian Moral Witness   183

Bibliography   200
Index   202

Preface

Changing Values is an attempt to present my understanding of some of the central principles of Christian moral thought. I believe that these represent the true centre of Christian morality; but they are articulated to meet some of the questions of our own age. They are old principles, and as such familiar — but I have tried to express them so as to meet today's questions.

Most of what is of lasting worth I have learned from Paul Ramsey and Oliver O'Donovan. It hardly needs saying that there is far more in their writings that I could ever encompass. In other words, I have learned much from studenrs at Trinity College over the last decade. The college has been a consistently positive place in which to work and to learn, and I am pleased to record my gratitude to all who made the college such a rich part of my life.

There are three people to whom I owe specific debts. Linda Woodhead made particularly helpful suggestions. David Sprackling offered many detailed comments, with great care and insight. More generally Sue Rose gave both encouragement and honest responce throughout the period of writing and rewriting. To them and to many others, I am truly grateful.

David Attwood
Prenton.

Introduction

This book aims to explain a particular understanding of Christian morality: Christian ethics. It outlines a moral theory, based on Christian faith. In offering a 'theory' of morality, the claim being made is that morality is basically to be understood. It is a matter of reasoned understanding, rather than being a matter of feeling, or decision, or will, or choice. And although moral truth has a real authority, such authority is reasonable, not arbitrary. Its authority does not simply impose itself by fiat or power, nor is it simply to be taken on trust.

Christian Ethics in a Changing World

The approach to morality that we will explore is that of Christian faith. There are, of course, many versions of Christian morality. Then there are debates about whether and how far Christian morality should be revised and updated. Are Christian traditions about marriage, or about warfare (for instance) open to change? How far is the Bible still relevant? Is the authority of the individual conscience paramount? There is even more divergence about basic theological and philosophical issues. Morality is on the agenda for all sorts of reasons. In particular, modern liberal society asks all sorts of unsettling questions about traditional beliefs and customs — and these questions are asked both by philosophers and by unruly teenagers. Many of these questions are also mirrored in theological debates.

In one sense this is a highly ambitious book, in that it aims to explain a perspective for any moral question. But in order to achieve this, it is quite a limited book. It is confined to one particular approach to ethics, with no more than glances at other theories. It looks at some 'issues', such as marriage, property, truth, but none of these is covered fully or at any length. The idea is simply that they should serve to illustrate and explain the theory. Nor is there any aim to solve 'ethical dilemmas', though reasons are given for seeing the existence of dilemmas as an inevitable and unthreatening aspect of human life.

The particular Christian theory that we will explore is relevant to wider secular debates about morality. The secular moralities of the Western world owe a great deal to Christian thought and Christian tradition. We will emphasise a number of features which secular thinking has inherited from Christianity — a conviction about the importance of reason, the view that every human being is of value, and that there is true goodness in the way we are.

However, whether these points of contact exist or are convincing, our study will be centred on a view of morality that lies at the heart of the Christian tradition and the church's teaching. It aims to work out the implications of fundamental Christian beliefs (in the love of God, in the creation of the world by God, in the defeat of evil, for instance). This tradition remains very close to general human apprehensions of the difference between good and evil. From a Christian point of view, this is no coincidence, because our sense of right and wrong derives ultimately from our creation in the image of God. This supports the claim that understanding Christian ethics more clearly is also a good way to understand everyday morality better.

From time to time we will compare Christian morality with some other current moral approaches. But perhaps one point should be clarified first. The question that is fundamentally being addressed is the question 'What should I do? How should I live?' This is not the same question as determining what social regulation there should be. The moral and legal areas are related, but they are not the same. Nor is the immediate issue that of asking what should be done about, say, the confusion of family life. There are moral aspects in handling the many social issues caused by the freedoms and problems of family life. But tackling the moral puzzle is our first concern. Understanding moral truth may help approach these questions, but they are different questions.

As I have said, we will focus on a theory of morality. A theory is not morality itself. It may seem rather dry, like a plan, or a skeleton. But without an understanding of the underlying anatomy, it is very hard to get a clear understanding of specific questions. So this is not exactly a theory which will explain 'How to take moral decisions' or 'How to solve moral dilemmas'. Indeed, one of the virtues of a good theory is that it can accept that there are some dilemmas which are not readily solved. But the theory will help us to understand why. It can also help us to distinguish between genuine moral dilemmas, and ordinary moral confusion or moral wilfulness.

The Moral Puzzle

It is wrong to dodge a rail fare, to evade income tax, not to return a library book. It is good to keep a promise, to pay a debt, to play golf honestly. Most people would agree on all these things. But what makes those things right or wrong, good or bad? And what does it mean when we say something is right or wrong? It's not easy to answer these questions.

There is something puzzling about our experience of morality. The puzzle is this. We know that there is a sharp difference between right and wrong, which we cannot do without. At the same time, we have very little confidence about the basis for that difference. What do '**Right**' and '**Wrong**' mean, and where do they come from?

Looked at one way, we cannot mistake the differences between gentleness and violence, between love and hatred, between care and cruelty, between honesty and deceit. It is simply wrong to abuse, beat and kill a child; it is good to care for a child with love and affection. There is no mistaking the contrast. It is only one example among many of the clear-cut nature of morality.

But looked at another way, we have enormous difficulty in agreeing about morality. Where does the sense of morality come from, and what does it rest on? Is there a source of moral authority, and if so, what is it? Is morality, alternatively, something which is felt, and willed, by individuals and society? Is it a matter of personal choice? Or is it a matter of social choice, which then becomes established in a society and its traditions and way of life? There are many possible answers to these questions. The variety of views leads not only to confusion, but also to debate which can easily become angry, bitter and even violent. In the end if there is no agreed basis for discussion, our decisions become a matter of dogma rather than rational persuasion. That is why this puzzle about morality is so important. For the apparently philosophical difficulties lead only too quickly to serious differences in what is seen to be right and wrong.

My conviction is that Christian faith can provide a convincing account of the moral puzzle. This book aims to provide such an account. In seeing how Christian morality works, we will find good foundations for traditional moral views. This is not to say that all moral dilemmas can be 'solved', and we will see why not. The point is that morality's clear distinction between right and wrong need not prevent us from clear and sensitive analysis. We do not have to choose between moral rigour and intelligent handling of difficult contemporary questions. It must be admitted that Christian moralists have not always succeeded in holding these two concerns together. Sometimes, they have so emphasized moral rigour, the hard and fast nature of moral distinctions, that moral complexities have been badly oversimplified. Perhaps in reaction to this, there has seemed recently to be such an emphasis on moral complexity that all moral clarity has been lost, or at best, very blurred.

Fascinating and Frustrating Dilemmas

We are fascinated and frustrated by the difficulty of morality. We are fascinated, as we would be by any puzzle. Surely, we think, there should be some way of finding at least some good answers to the questions we ask.

Occasionally we do find and agree an answer. An example might be the issue of the possible legitimacy of chemical and biological weapons in war. Could these weapons be a legitimate addition to military armouries? There might, after all, be something to say for weapons which do not kill but only disable for a period of time. But this possible advantage has been overruled by a general awareness of the mutual dangers of using such 'weapons', which are perhaps better called poisons. Although the use of chemical weapons is by no means unknown, nobody so far as I know claims that their use is morally legitimate. Here is a potential moral dilemma which has been solved. But there are many more instances of moral dilemmas which we do not seem able to solve in such a way. We feel as if we are in a **moral maze**, to borrow the title of a successful radio programme.

Our fascination turns to frustration when we find either that we can see no clear answers, or that if we do, we have simply no way of convincing those who disagree with us. This was seen, for instance, in debates on the age of consent for homosexuals. On one side, gay men claimed their rights to equality with heterosexuals, while on the other side, many pointed to the need to protect those young men who are deeply confused about their personal and sexual identity as they approach adulthood. Both had a moral concern, but there seemed no way in which the two concerns could meet on the same ground. The frustration caused by such stand-offs typically leads to anger, especially in this case, where gays saw their identity being denied by their opponents.

Fascination with moral dilemmas gives power to many story lines in soap operas and detective drama. One of the most popular is the recurring theme of the 'bad' detective who catches the wrongdoer by illegal means. Plots which use this theme gain interest from the way in which good and bad are seen to be mixed, especially in those who are supposed to be good. As we follow the twists and turns of the plot, we are expected to ask how valid our distinctions between good and bad really are. Can we actually disentangle right from wrong? In the detective story, this question gains power because the distinction between right and wrong is wholly indispensable. Without a clear sense of the wrongness of the crime to be solved, the whole plot would have very little point in the first place.

It is also significant that most fictional detectives have a near hundred per cent success rate. This is wildly unrealistic, but it is an essential element, which reassures the audience that good does indeed triumph over evil. So when this reassurance is questioned by the deliberate reversal of the good character of the detective, dramatic tension and irony can be powerfully increased.

As in detective fiction, we cannot do without the fundamental difference between right and wrong, good and bad. It is necessary to society, and it is necessary for each individual as well. But it is not enough to say we need morality, for we must offer good reasons for believing in moral truth. We need a rationale for our moral convictions. This book will offer a theory of morality which can provide such a rationale.

Changing or Unchanging Values?

We live in an age of changing **values.** This is true in family and sexual matters, in politics, in ecology, and in many other areas where new questions are constantly raised and debated. But it is only part of the truth. We also rely on some unchanging values — respect for life, liberty, fairness, basic honesty, and so on. Part of the argument of this book is that we need to find better foundations for the unchanging values. If we can understand those better, we may be better placed to respond to new questions, to areas of debate and change.

At the same time, there is another plea, not simply for unchanging values, but about the language of morality. The words 'unchanging' and 'values' do not belong all that happily together. Values are assigned, they are chosen, they are decided, more than they are given in the nature of things. The conviction of this book is that morality is indeed given in the nature of things. There are structures in the world, and in God's purposes. So it is more appropriate to talk of a framework for morality, than of a number of moral values. We cannot just assume, as many people do, that 'morality' and 'values' are interchangeable words. We begin by exploring some implications of using the language of 'values'.

One

Everyday Morality: Values

It is not easy to give a clear description of everyday moral beliefs. Most people's views are a partly consistent mixture of rules, maxims, and general principles. One feature of everyday morality in particular makes it hard to summarise with clarity, and that is the emphasis on the freedom of the individual to determine their own moral values.

Many people believe that morality is wholly subjective, a matter for the individual conscience. Morality is an attitude learned as we grow up, normally in the first instance through our relationship with our mother. As we discover her disapproval of some things, so we learn to regard them as bad or wrong. But according to this view, there is nothing which can be said to be objectively wrong, only things which we learn to regard as wrong. Of course, such subjective morality need not remain a purely instinctive matter. We learn from others what is generally regarded as wrong, and we can endeavour to order our moral beliefs and convictions as rationally as possible.

Such ordering may take the form of some kind of utilitarianism; or of some kind of respect for people; or some kind of morality based on consistency and basic human equality. In the fascinating study of American life *Habits of the Heart,* Robert Bellah and his collaborators analyse some strands of everyday moral culture in America. They see **utilitarian individualism** and **expressive individualism** as the dominant modern moral outlooks. These are overlaid on two older traditions, the biblical and the republican. Individualism does not hold complete sway, but it is powerful and pervasive. In its utilitarian form, individualism is oriented around success, about self-improvement and doing well, whether this is defined in financial or career terms, or more subtly in marriage and family. Expressive individualism looks for a different kind of goal, perhaps best summed up as self-fulfilment. This will emphasise intellectual and sensual fulfilment as the path to happiness rather than material prosperity or success, financial security and so on.

Bellah's analysis gives an extended, substantial analysis of everyday morality in America. A much briefer critique of popular moral assumptions is offered by Brenda Almond, in an article 'Seven Moral Myths'.[1] These myths are ideas which she believes to be widespread, and often taught in British schools and colleges. Some of these myths are:

Relativism   'the view that right and wrong vary with the opin-
                    ions of various groups' (78).

Toleration   one must refrain from judgement of moral views I
                    believe to be wrong.

Neutrality   specific moral values cannot be taught, for all moral
                    education must be 'value-neutral'.

Majority view   'what the majority say or believe is the standard of
                    right and wrong' (81).

Liberalism   that liberal morality is merely moral permissiveness.

Against these myths, Almond insists that 'liberalism is a strong moral position including certain strong positive values' (83). The fundamental ethical values are the simple ones of commitment to truth, care for each other and compassion. 'Living by such values is a matter of commitment and choice — but nevertheless a rational commitment if it is based on recognizing the way in which these values are fitted and adapted to the optimum flourishing of human beings' (77). Almond's critique of much of today's moral thought and moral education is powerfully expressed and accurate. But it remains awkward for her to speak as if there were moral truth and falsehood, when she is quite explicit in her opinion that the moral life is a matter of commitment and choice. The point that this is a rational commitment does not alter the fact that liberal morality is based in the will. As such it can be more or less reasoned, but can never be a matter of truth.

---

[1] Page numbers quoted are from the article reprinted in *New Occasions Teach New Duties?*

The Language of Moral Values

One thing not commented on by Bellah or Almond is the use of the word 'value' as a basic term in ethics. The word is increasingly taken for granted in moral discussion. For instance, Almond comments that new moral issues 'Have contributed to putting *ethics or values* in the centre of the world's stage'.[2] But to speak as if 'ethics' and 'values' were interchangeable words overlooks important differences. As we will see, the language of values belongs very naturally with the moral myths she criticises so vigorously. Christian theologians often appear equally ready to treat 'ethics' and 'values' as interchangeable words. The book by a leading Scottish ethicist, Ian McDonald, titled *Christian Values: Theory and Practice in Christian Ethics Today*, gives a sophisticated account of Christian ethics, skilfully combining moral principles, natural law and appeal to consequences. But the language of values is nowhere questioned as the basic term of moral discussion.[3]

There are no doubt many reasons why much moral argument today is conducted in terms of moral values. Value language gives a way of discussing moral points of view with widely different rationales. Using value language we can compare points of view giving a high value to freedom or to justice, to reason or tradition. We can compare biblical values with Victorian values, or family values, or modern values, and so on. Taking moral values as the basic shared language of morality apparently enables one to express a wide range of different viewpoints and traditions in the same terms, so making discussion possible.

We need to examine the implications of the fact that value language has become so central. We must look at the difference it makes to the way we think about morality. Our interest is focused on what morality itself means, returning to the central contention that morality is to be understood more than chosen or decided. It is not so much that value language can lead to the wrong moral conclusions, as that it obscures the nature of moral truth. It is simply not possible to translate an

---

[2] Ibid., p. 76, my italics.
[3] See Chapter 1.

articulated moral tradition into the truncated language of values
without losing essential substance.

Two Advantages of Value Language

Before criticising 'value' as the basic term for morality, we must
look at some of the positives. First of all, our society is rightly
concerned that morality should be a matter of genuine personal
conviction. A moral action is not one which is made simply in
deference or obedience to authority. Authorities such as the State,
or the Church, should not dictate to free individuals what values
they should hold. The language of moral values makes the point
that we should each be conscientiously convinced about our own
moral beliefs. A truly moral act requires me to act from a true
willing of what is good. If, for instance, I tell the truth simply
because I know I will be in trouble if I do not, my behaviour
does not really spring from a proper regard for the truth in itself.
If I adopt the value of truth for myself, that will mean that I tell
the truth out of genuine appreciation for truth.

A second and central advantage of value language is that it
provides a way in which competing moral views can be discussed.
Let us take economics. Someone may choose low inflation as their
principal economic value; someone else may make low unemployment their chief economic value; while a third may say that the
priority is the provision of excellent health care and schools. These
preferences most often stem from incompatible moral–political
philosophies. By translating these into value terms, we at once
reveal the relevance of these differing roots, and offer a way of
comparing their implications. In our personal life, someone may
value faithfulness to family and friends, while another may make
personal fulfilment their chief value. One person may value truth
very highly, while another values compassion, and a third values
friendship. We are rightly conscious that at certain levels we need
to respect each other's religious and personal beliefs. While we
argue for the truth, the liberal tradition has rightly grasped the vital
point that people should not be coerced into denying sincerely

held personal convictions. Clearly there are limits to freedom of personal conscience, and we will return to the question of trying to identify them.

The Root Meaning of 'Value'

The language of values is particularly appropriate to an individualist society. It is also very appropriate to a society centred on pursuit of economic success. 'Value' itself is an economic term. The key definition runs: 'The material or monetary worth of a thing; the amount at which it may be estimated in terms of some medium of exchange or other standard of a like nature'.[4] This is the primary way in which the word is used, and it differs subtly from the definition given for the word as used in ethics: 'That which is worthy of esteem for its own sake; that which has intrinsic worth'. However, the dictionary offers a modern meaning for the word 'values' (first used in 1921) 'One's principles or standards; one's judgement of what is valuable or important in life'. These three connected definitions offer a helpful insight into the way in which value has come to be the central word of moral argument. The movement is from material worth, to moral esteem to principles, standards. Describing principles as values would be merely a matter of words. But then the word 'value' reaches back, as it were to the root meaning of the word, as a quantity in a medium of exchange. So principles become quantifiable, and one can then talk of the value of truth weighed against, say, the value of life.

That is to say, one person's principles, which may belong within a particular religious framework, are called 'their values'. These can then be compared with someone else's values, quite separately from considering the context within which those values originate.

Value language thus offers a moral medium of exchange, so to speak, within which different moralities can, as it were, be traded. There are advantages to this. It enables us to commend our own values, without appearing to commend, much less enforce, the whole package of belief underlying those values. Christian and other religious

---

[4] From the *Shorter Oxford English Dictionary*.

traditions can thus commend the value of human life, for instance, to a pluralist and secular society. We can encourage one another to live to high moral standards, without necessarily agreeing on what those standards are. Since we have assumed that nobody can be morally faulted for their choice of values, provided that they are reasonably consistent, we cannot easily prescribe and teach particular moral rules as given and non-negotiable. But we can teach that everyone should endeavour to live by their own sincerely chosen moral beliefs. In this way, we hope, high standards of moral behaviour are possible without agreement about what exactly that means.

Problems with the language of moral value

Value language has become so universally taken for granted, for reasons which are deep rooted in our basic liberal assumptions, that it is no doubt a forlorn hope to try to row against such a powerful current! There are, however, several concerns about what this means for the fabric of morality, and for society itself. In particular, we have to pursue the question raised a moment ago about the limits to personal moral freedom. Are there not certain non-negotiable moral values, which everybody ought to hold? It soon becomes clear there must be such values. However, the idea of non-negotiable values is in some ways self-contradictory. One of the problems that can arise from this self-contradiction is that society can become arbitrary and tyrannical in enforcing various moral values. Before we can explore this, we must consider whether morality can be properly expressed in value language.

It is important to consider what understanding may be obscured or even lost, if we lose the language to express it. At first sight it seems quite unproblematic to translate all sorts of moral statements into the language of values. The command 'Never tell a lie' becomes the value 'Truth is an absolute value'. The virtue of courage becomes the personal value of courage. 'Protecting the natural world' is rendered as 'The value of nature and the environment'. Any moral exhortation or goal or principle can be quite simply translated into value language in this kind of way. However, a great deal of understanding is liable to be lost when such a translation is made.

Values and Moral Reason

There are various problems. Essentially, they revolve around the point that value language belongs to an outlook where morality is decided upon, and chosen, rather than reasoned. When a moral rule is reduced (or translated) to a value, it becomes much harder to see how a rule works, in being understood and applied to different circumstances. Casuistry becomes even more difficult, or possibly incomprehensible.[5] To see why this is, we can turn to the example of truth-telling. 'Never tell a lie' might well be translated in value language as 'Truth is an absolute value' but there are occasions when we need to consider the possibility that truth is not an absolute value, that we do not impart all the truth we know, freely to any who ask. This possibility must be considered with respect to particular circumstances, to the relationships involved and so on. Let us consider an example of casuistry.

Suppose a counsellor promises confidentiality to her clients, since knowledge of things they tell her in counselling does not belong to anyone else. The counsellor might perhaps express this by saying that she gives a higher value to protecting her clients and her promises of confidentiality than to the value of sharing that knowledge with others who might have much good to gain from it. She might even say that she gave a higher value to confidentiality than to truth, if she were asked an unavoidable direct question. This would clearly be the right moral conclusion to draw. However, the language of values here serves to obscure the substance of her moral convictions. For it is not really the case that she values confidentiality more than truth, but that confidence is owed to her client, and the truth is not owed to the enquirer. The right moral decision depends on understanding the relationships involved. Without this understanding, the counsellor will have much greater difficulty when the structure of the situation changes. For instance, if she is told (in confidence) by a child about serious sexual abuse, or if an adult makes threats of suicide or murder, then the balance of confidentiality and truth-telling is likely to be decisively altered. Merely weighing values is not the way to think about such situations. Careful reasoning about the patterns of good and of relationship is needed.

---

[5] We will consider the importance of casuistry, and what it means, especially in Chapters 4 and 8.

There are problems too, for virtue and personal integrity. However much one allows that a 'virtue' can be considered as a 'value', the inevitable tendency is to look at the values to be considered and gained in other senses. For instance, suppose the possibility of telling a lie opens up some good for someone else. Considering the value to be gained by the other against the 'disvalue' of loss of integrity can only have one conclusion. For 'disvalue' cannot be weighed against some- one else's 'value'. Inevitably we are bound to weigh the good for someone else more highly than the gain for ourselves. This **weighing of values** one against the other simply does no justice at all to the proper processes of moral reason. If I decide not to tell a lie, and the result is that someone else suffers thereby, I am not thereby self-re- garding. Perhaps a lie in business can gain a contract, without which many will lose their jobs. Such a dilemma cannot be arbitrated simply by weighing conscience and virtue against the potentially lost jobs. The two kinds of things are simply incomparable. This is not to say that such a lie could never be justified, only that clear moral reasons would need to be shown why the lie should be told. Again, the point is not so much that one cannot use value language to describe a moral decision, but that working through moral questions using value language inevitably tends to obscure the substance of moral argument. Morally relevant considerations have to be artificially converted, as it were, into values.

Ends, Means and Values

The attempt to translate such questions into values inevitably distorts proper moral considerations. One distortion is that the consequences of our actions can come to seem much more important than the means we use to reach our goals. The possession and use of nuclear weapons provides an illustration of this (let us hope a dated one). In 1945 it seemed clear to President Truman that the use of the atom bombs on Hiroshima and Nagasaki would markedly shorten the war against Japan. The decision he took is still debated by historians. Would the Japanese have soon surrendered anyway? Were there other motives in the mind of the President, such as forestalling a Soviet advance?

Nevertheless, it remains quite a plausible case that, in terms of the foreseeable consequences alone, Truman's decision was justifiable. His belief that the bombs would end the war was vindicated, and many American lives were saved, together with the lives of many Japanese and other fighters. Nobody was in a position to take full account of the long drawn out effects of atomic fallout, along with the terrible destruction of the immediate blast. Yet the world is now all but unanimous in condemning the decision to drop the bombs. Such condemnation relies on the moral point that there are some things which should simply not be done, however great the goal that is sought. 'The end does not justify the means', we say, and rightly so. At the same time it needs also to be said that there are some means which are justified by their ends, and only by their ends. For if any war is to be fought for the sake of justice, peace and security, then only those ends can justify the combat and destruction involved.[6] But it is hard for value language, which inevitably tends to weigh the ends, to give a good account of the dynamic involved here. The moral discussion about ends and means is not a particularly easy one, and the inevitable tendency of value language is to make understanding the issues harder rather than easier.

Values and Preferences

Value language presents moral decisions as a **weighing of alternatives**, almost as if one was considering whether to value an Old Master painting more highly than a symphony orchestra, or a game of football as against a bottle of wine. In all these examples (though they have little else in common) there may be reasons or motives or preferences on either side. But in the end it is simply a matter of choice, of decision. The language of moral values presents moral thought as analogous to artistic or sporting preferences.

In making moral choices, we attribute a leading role to **conscience**.[7] It is here presented as a kind of inborn faculty, with a kind of instinct for discerning the highest moral values. Of course, just as

---

[6] The Just War tradition contains extensive discussion of these moral questions.
[7] The development of the concept of conscience is discussed in Chapter 13.

one can learn about art, football or wine, and learn more than on a first acquaintance, so one's moral palate can be educated, and one can become more discerning. But the analogy between art (for instance) and morality has a fatal flaw. The values of art, even if they could be clearly established, do not claim us in the way that basic moral values do. We rightly consider it vital that everyone should have a clear grasp of essential moral values. It is problematic if someone thinks that cheating is preferable to honesty. These are not moral alternatives, between which anyone is free to make their own choice.

The Language of Values

There are certain basic rights and wrongs in our treatment of other human beings. It is wrong to commit genocide. No other values can provide a justification for genocide, or for all sorts of other wrong actions. Genocide is wrong whatever those committing it believe, even if they sincerely and conscientiously believe it the right thing for the sake of some overriding cause. It is wrong even if laws are passed to 'legalise' such action in the nation concerned. It would be wrong even if there were no international law prohibiting genocide. Nor is genocide a case on its own in this respect. Premeditated murder, deliberate lying and cheating for selfish gain, careless breaking of solemn promises, lawless theft and vandalism — these and a host of other things are simply wrong. They remain wrong whether or not they are forbidden by law, whatever the person doing them believes. Such things are not open to moral choice or decision, for they are simply wrong.

How does value language handle this aspect of morality? At one level, there is no great problem. For it is perfectly possible to say that there are some values which everyone ought to hold. Brenda Almond argues like this when she says: 'The fundamental ethical values are not sectional: on the contrary, they acquire the status of being fundamental ethical values in virtue of their capacity to appeal to all as human beings, and not as members of any particular group'.[8] The most

---

[8] 'Seven Moral Myths', p. 77.

prevalent basis for everyday moral values is a conviction about the value of human beings, and that it is good for us to flourish, to be happy, integrated and so on. If people are to flourish, then their life and property must be respected, they deserve to know the truth, to have certain freedoms. They need a certain social order for their protection, so that they are not subject to arbitrary or violent actions by others, so that promise made to them are honoured, and so on. It is relatively straightforward to derive basic moral values from these needs for individual and social flourishing — values of truth, life, property, law, justice, etc.

This brings us from the variability of an individual set of moral values, to something that is beginning to look like an **objective moral code**. Such a code is also necessary for the health of society. Without some basic agreement about the moral tenets which underlie everyday life, and legislation too, social life becomes barely possible. Some objectivity in morals is necessary to society.

At the same time, a secular society is also bound to say that society is the basis for objective morality. At this point there has to be some counterweight to individualism. Rather than every individual being their own moral authority, morality gains objectivity through the moral authority of wider society. Society is seen as having evolved a moral code over the course of history, through continued discussion and experience. Such a code gains its authority through its adoption, its continued revision and refinement, its exposure to new circumstance and challenges, facing new contexts and opportunities. Appeal may perhaps be made to humanity, or the nation, or even the universe. Moral education assumes the highest possible profile, for there is really no other basis for moral knowledge (in the absence of any substantial basis in reason or religion).

Leaning the whole weight of moral objectivity on society has some very real dangers, especially when people are anxious about falling moral standards and a sense of social insecurity. Here are some of the dangers which we must consider: the danger of arbitrariness; the problem of moral moderation and forgiveness; the danger of rigidity; the risk of placing too much weight on publicity and public knowledge; and the risk of underrating individual freedom.

declining values.

The arbitrary nature of purely social morality

The first cluster of potential problems arises from the similarity of a socially legitimated morality to the sense of public moral self right-eousness found in major criminal trials. Of course this is not what is intended by the theory that society is the source of moral objectivity.

But it is only a short step from saying that something should not be done because the moral authority of society forbids it, to saying that public disapproval forbids it. Society needs to draw and maintain boundaries to define what is socially acceptable behaviour. However, these boundaries are often considerably affected by the emotional factors involved. Such emotions are strong, and no doubt play an important and at times valuable role in social discipline. In giving publicity to crime, or moral failure, and its just reward, we discourage such behaviour. But these emotions always risk under-valuing the need for reason and moderation. The feelings of public vengeance have a simple clear-cut, right or wrong feel to them. They can be rigid and arbitrary in condemning some perceived wrongs, while overlooking others altogether. Notoriously, those feeling such emotions find the idea of forgiveness extremely difficult to encompass.

We can perhaps find examples of socially driven morality in the reaction to the question of single women with unwanted pregnan-cies. For good reasons, such pregnancies are considered problematic. Young single mothers are often not well suited to bringing up young children, for several reasons. They may lack emotional maturity; unmarried, they lack the full support of the child's father; they are very likely to be financially dependent, probably poor and ill-housed. It is hardly surprising that statistics show that such children are likely to fare badly in education, in employment, and other ways. A cluster of moral reactions is seen in social response to this issue. There is the choice between **abortion** and bearing the child. Many who would condemn abortion as the taking of human life nevertheless express a more obvious disapproval for those who actually bear the child. A child is visible in public life in a way that an abortion is not. Indeed, the lack of provision for such children is partly responsible for the frequency of abortion. There is considerable social disapproval of such single mothers. It is hard to find social expression for forgiveness, even for those who may be much more sinned against than sinning. On the other hand, social morality has always had a much more ambivalent attitude to the fathers of such children. On the one hand there is the strong feeling that they should play a responsible part in supporting the women and children. On the other hand, notoriously, there is the sense that boys will be boys and that it is up to women to watch out for themselves. Mingled with this is the sneaking male admiration for those who manage to get away with it. Here is certainly a considerable degree of arbitrariness. Whatever the precise balance of these reactions, the issue illustrates the dangers of relying too simply on socially-generated moral reactions. It is much rarer, for instance, for the problem of teenage pregnancies to lead society to question its own sexual morality. Yet sexual morality is one of the main roots of the problem. Of course teenage pregnancies have always occurred in societies with the most severe sexual moralities. But the current emphasis on sexual fulfilment and sexual freedom is quite obviously part of the context in which the scale of unwanted pregnancies has to be understood.

The other area of difficulty for making society the authority for morality is that the content of morality comes to depend on whatever is given public approval or disapproval at any particular time. Two things at least tend to follow from this. There is, for one thing, the age-old temptation to behave badly if we think that nobody will notice and that we will get away with it. Psalm 53 is aimed at those who behave badly because they believe there is no God, and in Psalm 10 evil men are portrayed as saying God will never notice. But if our morality does not depend at all on belief in God, but only on belief in society, the temptation to underplay wrongdoing is that much stronger. In a curious way, making morality objective by appealing to social backing can be almost less convincing than appealing to the individual conscience. Religious belief offers much greater resources for relating objective moral truth to the personal conviction of the individual than does a socially derived morality. In Christian thought, at any rate, religious beliefs about God's love and grace undergird the appeal to personal response and responsibility. It is not nearly so clear if and how a morality based on social evolution can provide moral resources. Perhaps in normal everyday life it is not problematic to be faithful and truthful with those who are near to us. But it is much less clear how such a foundation for morality can lead us to behave well when the rewards for doing so are in doubt.

Social morality depends on public pronouncement and social control

Our society places a heavy stress on moral pronouncements, condemnations of acts we disapprove, and so on. Social approval of good behaviour is increasingly significant in a society which can depend less and less on the moral legacy of religious belief. This is one of the factors which helps to explain the shrill tone of media moralising. Along with the call for a renewal of moral values seems to go a powerful barrage of moral exhortation. This exhortation takes many forms — strident denunciations, moral pressure groups, searching media investigation of the private lives of public individuals. It is also noteworthy that society is much better at denouncing what is wrong, than praising what is right.[9]

Another feature associated with a belief in the social nature of morality is likely to be a heavy emphasis on forms of social control. Measures of social control and surveillance no doubt arise first in response to particular fears about crime or particular forms of injustice or immorality. But they can only be sustained in a social context where it is believed that certain kinds of behaviour offend against moral or social norms. Interesting examples of this kind can be seen in changing social beliefs over the last generation, say from 1960 to the present day. In 1960 there was still a good deal of control over young people with regard to their sex lives. By and large, many adults thought it wrong to allow students (for instance) easy opportunities for sexual activity.[10] Access of women to men's accommodation, and vice versa, was typically limited in some respects. In 1997, the accepted morality of sexual activity is considerably changed. The moral emphasis now is on contraception and prevention of sexually transmitted diseases

---

[9] I owe this observation to David Sprackling. His comment is surely borne out by the well-known difficulty of making 'good news' interesting.

[10] The change in the age of majority is no doubt both cause and effect of this characteristic shift in attitudes.

(including AIDS). The point is that patterns of supervision and control are clearly related to prevalent moral convictions. A change in the opposite direction has taken place with regard to smoking. Discovery of the health risks of smoking has made smoking in many contexts morally unacceptable. Along with this, people who would not dream of rebuking a stranger for almost any other private behaviour will be prepared to enforce 'no smoking' notices! The level of supervision and social control that is exercised bears witness to certain moral convictions about health as well as the fears we have about the health risks of cigarette smoke.

Conclusion

Talking about morality only in terms of values is unsatisfactory. The question is: do we have any choice? There are many complexities in moral discussion, and these are precisely the complexities which a language of moral values aims to avoid. Is there another way to handle these questions? The old simple truths of Christian moral thought appear not to give us the guidance we need.[11] The main argument of this book is that they can indeed provide the resources for a framework of Christian ethics. Such a framework needs to be carefully articulated in order to be ready to answer new questions, or old questions put in new ways. Before we begin to bring these materials together, it will be helpful to look at some of the complexities of moral questions. How can these complexities be given their full weight, while at the same time holding on to the clear simplicities of morality?

---

[11] That is, of course, as we think we have received them from the tradition.

Two

Simplicity and Complexity

Our generation has become particularly impressed with the difficulty of moral issues. Many people are confused, not seeing any way to reconcile a sharp distinction between good and evil with the real dilemmas which they encounter and hear about. Others become cynical, and deny that there is, after all, any sharp distinction between right and wrong, seeing only a continuum from one end of the scale to the other. Many decisions, they would say, fall into a large grey area of mixed good and bad.

However, the existence of difficult moral dilemmas does not lessen the fundamentally sharp distinction between good and evil. The existence of twilight does not disprove the existence of night and day. In order to explore this, we first consider some of the main ways in which moral issues can get complicated.

Five Moral Complexities

a) The meaning of moral categories

There are, of course, several sorts of question which can complicate moral issues. One is that of deciding how to apply a particular moral rule, finding out precisely what it means. The example of truth and fiction provides an illustration of this, though not one which causes difficulty very often. But the question of whether a 'white' lie, a harmless lie told to protect someone's feelings, for instance, is a morally forbidden type of lie is often debated.

Many moral debates, like this, depend on working out what a given moral category includes. How are we to define 'human life', 'marriage' and 'private property' from a moral perspective? The central meanings are not in question. But when does life begin? When does it end? Again, we usually have little trouble in saying whether a couple is married. But there are several disputed categories. For instance, some maintain that divorce is in effect impossible because marriage vows bind husband and wife until death. This bond remains even though the relationship itself effectively comes to an end through separation, remarriage, and so on. Similarly, the everyday understanding of private property is not in dispute. But what are the limits of private property, if any? What responsibilities do large scale ownership of private property entail?

b) The clash of duties

More often than not, moral debates concern more than one moral principle at the same time. The clash of competing principles provides the most obvious kind of moral dilemma. Does loyalty to a friend override the duty to tell the truth, or the other way round? Should we tell a lie to save a friend from trouble? Should a woman have an abortion to try to save her marriage? These are the characteristic dilemmas of soap operas, and they are real enough, even if not occurring as frequently as they do on screen. On a global scale, the question of nuclear deterrence seems to involve a clash of duties. Is it right to threaten massive destruction in order to preserve peace and security? Or is that threat so wrong that no good cause can justify it?[1]

Some writers suggest that we should attempt to form a hierarchy of moral duties. We might say, perhaps, that life is more important than truth, and truth than property. Others argue that if our duties are rightly understood there will be no ultimate clashes. We will follow neither of these suggestions. Instead, we will see that moral questions can only be clarified by a more searching inquiry. Such inquiry must include the features of each particular dilemma, and the basic meaning of the moral principles at issue. We will find that this can often clarify the dilemma, though it must also be admitted that our lives can be so complex that some dilemmas finally admit no really effective answer.

---

[1] It seems to me plausible to suggest that this apparently insoluble dilemma, which was particularly acute in the 1960s, contributed greatly to a loss of confidence in moral truth.

c) Dealing with moral failure

Sometimes, the dilemmas we find ourselves in are a result of wrong-doing already committed, whether by us or by others. War is one obvious area where this is true. After all, if people were not greedy, aggressive, and untrustworthy there would be no need for war. Perhaps, if love really ruled in all things, there would be no broken marriages. Divorce, with all its pain as well as its new possibilities, would set no more quandaries.

Setting right things that we have done wrong can bring its own moral problems. For instance, if we have let someone down in a way they knew nothing about, it may be quite wrong to tell them all about it. On the other hand, it may be quite wrong to continue to keep it a secret from them. Suppose, perhaps, that a manager obtains a substantial contract, on which many people's jobs subsequently depend, by means that are morally dubious but legally borderline. If that manager repents at a later date, it may be quite disloyal to many people to make a clean breast of it all. But it would be easy to envisage circumstances in which continued secrecy only made things worse. Similar moral problems arise when there is a conflict of interests between people, or a conflict of loyalties to different people.

Nobody who has any awareness of the complexity of human lives and relationships would claim to be able to 'solve' such problems. But we should not deduce from this that morality is confused or self-contradictory. The fact that loyalty to people whom we wish to protect may clash with the duty to tell the truth does not deny the reality of either moral claim. It does not threaten the fabric of our moral convictions. Clearly, the problem is to be located in the way in which our lives so often become entangled in a variety of claims and failures.

d) The problem of motive

There is another type of obscurity in our moral discernments. Moral judgement has to recognise the complexity of human action. As we say, we can do the right thing for the wrong reason. We can also do something wrong without realising, or without intending to do wrong. To some extent, the questions involved in discerning someone's inward disposition can be separated from the question of what is right to do. For instance, someone may behave very generously, not out of kindness but out of a desire to be well thought of. The motive does not match the deed, but that does not make generosity itself a bad thing. However, there are also occasions when the inward intention does actually enter into the discernment of what should be done. A doctor caring for a dying patient should intend to relieve the patient's pain, but should not intend to kill the patient as a means to that end. In this field, finely balanced but crucial moral judgements can only be made with reference to the doctor's intentions.

e) New moral issues

The last sort of moral complication we will mention here has to do particularly with the rapid changes and discoveries of the modern age. Part of understanding Christian ethics is to do with understanding the realities of our lives. In a day when human institutions, and social and cultural assumptions of all kinds are constantly reviewed and challenged, morality seems also to be changing. Is there a substantial reality to our moral beliefs? The point is not that morality actually changes, but that it has to be made relevant to the new circumstances of our lives.

A time traveller to our century might suppose that we had managed to overcome the law of gravity, when he saw our single-span bridges, our planes and helicopters, our toy balloons filled with helium. We would laugh at such a misunderstanding. But those who claim that the Just War tradition is of no use in a nuclear age actually make a similar mistake. Of course, Just War theory was devised in a different time, but its moral insights into the nature of earthly justice and peace, into the use of force and power in politics, and so on, are abiding insights. In so far as they are true, they remain fundamentally relevant to questions raised by nuclear technology. In a similar way, medical technology raises new questions about the way we should protect human life. To understand the moral aspects, we will need to grasp the new technologies, and we may have to understand the moral fundamentals in new ways as well.

We have considered five general areas of moral complexity:

(a) Clarifying the meaning of moral categories.
(b) The clash of moral duties.

(c)   Ambiguities arising from clashing interests, and from past moral failure.

(d)   The obscurities of human inwardness (intentions and motives) in judging human actions.

(e)   Questions raised by new technologies and other changes.

Of course this is nothing like an exhaustive list. It also needs to be remembered that the complexities we are usually confronted with do not fall neatly into one or other of these rough areas, but involve several different difficulties at the same time. But it is always important to try to analyse and understand such difficulties. Without analysis, we have little chance of seeing how the clear and simple contrast between good and evil can be intelligently related to the real complexities which we experience.[2]

As well as considering the complex side of moral issues, we also need to think about what we mean when we talk of a simple distinction between right and wrong. To begin with, there is something non-negotiable about morality. Moral truth challenges us, it asks us to choose between right and wrong. The contrast is strong, the distinction basic and simple. It is embodied in apparently simple rules like 'Do not kill', 'Do not hate', and 'Do not steal'. Here we must be careful. If the things which complicate morality can be simplified, then it is sometimes necessary to look more carefully at the apparently simple things. The 'simple' commandments of **Judaeo–Christian morality** need to be understood more deeply. Asking what a moral rule means, for instance, is not quibbling. It is crucially important, and it leads us in two different directions. One way, it leads us to ask about the rationale for moral commands, where they come from; and the other way, it asks us to think quite hard about how a moral rule can apply to the real issues we have just sketched.

Morality is Objective

Essentially, the difference between good and bad has to do with the nature of reality. That which is good accords with the nature of things

---

[2] We will not try to find quick 'answers' for these five areas. They form the background; all will be considered in one way or another.

as they reflect the goodness of God and his good purposes for his creation. The most important thing about God's goodness is his love. God's love is therefore the first test of right and wrong. It is God's love which gives us the pattern for our love and for our standards of right and wrong. The second test of what is right and good is that it should be a true fulfilment of God's purpose and design in creation. The two themes of **love** and **creation** form the heart of our exploration of the many aspects and complexities of morality. It is fundamentally these two themes which provide the basis for saying that morality is both given and reasonable. Its authority makes sense because it is based on the nature of things. It is not an arbitrary authority.

The fact that morality is based on objective truths means that morality has an objective quality. But we have to ask whether the objectivity of morals can be defended by referring to supposedly objective Christian faith. Many would argue that anything which is an element of Christian faith is only a personal, subjective, belief. In what way does making faith the foundation for morality establish the objectivity of morals? We can make this claim because Christian belief itself claims to be a true interpretation of the way the world is. In this sense, faith is just as objective as belief in the evolution of species, or the Big Bang. This is not to say that these are the same kinds of belief, or that the evidence for them is of the same kind. But not all beliefs are simply 'subjective'. Most beliefs relate reasonably directly to some objective facts. Of course, we are not dealing here with the more marginal aspects of faith, but with its central themes. There is plenty of evidence on the nature of love, and of the pattern of the created world. It is not all that big a step from the evidence of love to the Christian beliefs which we are appealing to.

The **objectivity of morals** means that morality is not imposed by the will of society, let alone by the will of the individual. Morality is very arbitrary when it is a matter of personal choice and decision. So, for instance, someone may defend their right to deceive anyone outside their own particular circle. Or again, sexual morality can very quickly be reduced to a level where whatever feels right is pronounced right by the person concerned. Someone may decide not to pay any regard to the feelings of others, in the name of their own feelings or self-fulfilment. In a somewhat similar way, social morality can seem to depend on what is found to be generally acceptable or popularly desired. One sometimes gets an impression that those who wish to see a change in the moral climate feel that what is socially acceptable thereby becomes morally legitimate. For instance, public opinion seems to be the only restraint on some scientists conducting research into human conception — or at least the only attention they are prepared to give to morality.

In contrast with a subjective view, whose moral lines are only drawn in sand, an objective morality recognises some definite lines. The difference between right and wrong is sometimes a clear straight line. One act of theft, or deceit, or hatred, is recognisably like another, and unlike acts of honesty and kindness. To point to such clear and sharp distinctions is not to deny that there are also ambiguities. Nor is it to deny that the distinction has to be enquired into afresh in new situations. New methods of operating stock markets give, perhaps, new ways of gaining unfair financial advantages, which shade over into deceit or theft. But it is quite possible to disentangle new questions like this: we have to relate the new realities to what the old distinctions intended. We have to understand more deeply, not make arbitrary choices or take a vote. Here we come to one of the key themes of understanding ethics in the modern age. Morality is essentially about some simple and clear differences. But those differences have to be properly related to complex as well as simple circumstances.

The apparent simplicity of moral boundaries is not at odds with careful handling of real complexity. In practice, we are all quite well used to handling examples of this. Everyone, including quite young children, can easily understand the difference between fiction and real life. In real life, respect for the truth means that we do not invent what we say, for that would be lying. But in fiction, everything is invented. Fiction has its own rules and conventions, and in certain ways also aims to respect and uncover truth. We do not regard the difference between fact and fiction as paradoxical or problematic. In this respect, and this is only one example, our simple contrast between truth telling and lying is in fact quite sophisticated. The rule 'always tell the truth' must either be rephrased, or the implicit assumption made that this does not apply to story-telling. There are of course innumerable assumptions like this which we take for granted, but which have important moral implications. This means that we often have to take a good deal of care to ensure that we say exactly what we mean when we are trying to draw any particular moral boundary.

We can use an analogy from the laws of physics. The physical law of gravity is essentially simple. But its operation is sometimes simple, sometimes less so. It is not easy to explain why a spinning top may appear to defy the law of gravity! But the spinning top does not disprove gravity. No more do the existence of complex cases and undeniably 'grey' areas deny the difference between right and wrong.

Are Objective Rules too Restrictive?

Adherence to clear moral boundaries is frequently thought of as restrictive. It seems that definite prohibitions must inhibit our freedom, and that there is a risk that drawing moral lines will actually prevent us from achieving or being the best. If this is most often said and felt about sexual ethics, it is also true of other areas. Moral boundaries may appear to be overly restrictive in politics; they may seem harsh and arbitrary in medical research. In particular, it can appear that rules actually hinder the purposes which they were originally intended to serve. This concern has loomed large in Christian moral arguments for a generation.

Essentially, we will find that it forces us to understand the basic structure of moral argument more deeply. We are driven back to the fundamental themes of love and creation. The order of creation gives us reason to see that there are underlying continuities in life. One marriage is recognisably like another in certain ways; human life should always be respected because each individual bears the image of God. One central aspect of love is our faithful respect for one another. So our lives lived in love should be trustworthy, reliable; especially at some of the critical junctures. The doctrines of love and creation provide the impetus for finding the right boundaries of morality, and insisting on them.

One of the dangers of clear and objective rules is that they can be applied in too literal a way, to situations for which they were not intended. People are often prone to think that if they have 'kept the rule', then they have done all that is morally required. By the same token, we condemn others for breaking rules, when we do not have the whole picture. The twin dangers of **legalism** and **moralism**[3] are very real, if we make moral rules a substantial part of our outlook. However, the way to avoid these dangers is not simply to ditch the rules. The proper way of avoiding legalism is to understand the rules, and their purpose, more clearly. Rules can then be applied intelligently. When difficulties arise, we can go back to the underlying rationale, to see what the purpose of the rule is.

Moral Simplicity and Complexity

The essential simplicity of morality is the stark contrast between right and wrong, between good and bad. This difference derives from the fact that God is good, and his creation is good, and his loving purpose is good. Human participation in this goodness is not automatic, for it is a matter of conscious, willing and rational agreement with God. It is possible for human beings to mistake God's purposes, or defy them more or less explicitly. The difference between right and wrong is grounded in the difference between following God's purposes and not doing so.

At the same time, God's love and his creation are full of different realities and possibilities. While there is a clear difference between telling the truth and telling lies, knowing and expressing the whole truth is not something that can be encompassed by human beings. For instance, it is a commonplace of modern psychology and ancient philosophy that we never fully understand the truth about ourselves. How much less can we hope to understand everything about other people. We should not be surprised, then, if we find that there are occasions when it is difficult to find the right way of telling the truth, even about quite limited incidents. This means, for instance, that moral understanding cannot be contained in moral

---

[3] For a discussion of moralism and legalism, see Chapter 8. The point developed there is essentially that too rigid an adherence to the moral letter fails to understand moral thought by divorcing the moral rule from its rationale.

rules and principles. The fact that the rules do not do our work for us is not a reason for complaining at them. It just means that we have to think hard about what they mean, perhaps in the same way as a physicist has to think hard about how the law of gravity applies to the spinning top.

In the next few chapters we will examine the fundamental aspects of our knowledge of **God's purposes**. These are the doctrines of God's love and of creation. We will sketch them separately and then together. They provide the basis on which we can clarify some typical moral questions. We will look at some general issues, such as the role of conscience, the Bible's moral instruction, the use of moral rules, legalism, and forgiveness. Along the way, we will consider some specific topics, such as property, sexuality and marriage, euthanasia, justice and legislation. These are inevitably a scattered selection, but they will help to put flesh on some of the more theoretical points. They will help us to see how it is possible to understand moral truth, even as it exerts its claim on us.

Three

Christian Love, the Foundation for Christian Ethics

One side of the puzzle of ethics is the simplicity of moral truth. We long to see things as either good or bad, either right or wrong. Of course we do not look for such simple distinctions everywhere, but morality seems to call for them. Not all our choices are moral choices. To think about money, for instance, it is not (usually) a moral choice whether I buy a pair of shoes or have an evening out. But it is a moral choice whether I try to steal a pair of shoes, or defraud someone else of their savings.

Where does this simple distinction between right and wrong come from? Is it simply a distinction imposed by human minds, trying to find some secure way of understanding the world and our actions within it? In **Christian ethics** there is a good reason to think that this distinction is genuine and true. The basis for the distinction can certainly be expressed in several different ways. We can say that what we do is or is not in accordance with God's will. Or we can say that what we do reflects the goodness of God, or belongs within his purposes for us. We can give all of these ideas more substance by relating them to the love of God.

If we ask whether something we do reflects God's love, we can quite quickly give a lot of content to the distinction between good and bad, right and wrong. Love is the strong central point of Christian ethics. Of course love can be described in many different ways. This chapter will outline some of the key aspects of Christian love.

The love of God is the central theme of the New Testament. Jesus came to proclaim the message 'God is Love', a message which he lived out himself. He lived it not only in his teaching, not only in his work of healing, but also in the company he kept. He was not afraid to be associated with the least respectable. God's love is shown in his attitude to those who made themselves God's enemies, not just those who claimed God as on their side. In the death of Jesus we see the love of God at its fullest. 'Jesus died that we might live' has been the claim and the belief of Christian believers ever since.

Christians see in God's love the pattern to imitate in their own lives. The love of God experienced by the Christian provides the mainspring for Christians to love God and love their neighbour. Christians are motivated by the recognition that the only appropriate response to God's love is to return that love. Since Jesus died for those who were not law-abiding, not respectable or pure, Christians need not fear that moral failure will separate them from God. Doing what is right follows from being already accepted by God; it is not an attempt to win God's acceptance.

Christian living is not determined by a rule-book. The fundamental motivation for good behaviour is love, and love also determines the shape of morality. The moral rules follow from the knowledge that there are some things that love will never do, some qualities which it will always display. The acid test of any action is finally always 'is it loving?' Jesus underlined this in the most emphatic way. He brought together two sayings from the Pentateuch. He followed Jewish teaching, which identified as the most important commandment 'Love the Lord your God with all your heart, with all your soul and with all your mind' (Deut. 6:5). He coupled it with a less prominent verse 'Love your neighbour as you love yourself' (Lev. 19:18). These two sayings provide the framework for all 'the law and the prophets', in other words, the whole Jewish moral tradition enshrined in the Old Testament.

The theme of love is so prominent in the thought of Jesus, especially as expressed by the Gospel of John, that we cannot overemphasise it. One or two sayings will make this clear enough. At the last supper, shortly before his death, Jesus dwells on the theme: 'And now I give you a new commandment: love one another. As I have loved you, so you must love one another'. In the Sermon on the Mount, we find this: 'You have heard that it was said, "Love your friends, hate your enemies". But now I tell you: love your enemies and pray for those who persecute you, so that you may become the sons of your Father in heaven' (Matt. 5:43–45).

It is perhaps sayings like this which have led some people to think that there is a huge contrast between Jesus and the Old Testament. We should notice, though, that the phrase 'Hate your enemies' does not come from the Old Testament. On the contrary, the Old Testament is also saturated with the theme of the love of God. It was out of love that God chose the people of Israel: 'But the Lord loved you and wanted to keep the promise that he made to your ancestors. That is why he saved you by his great might and set you free from slavery to the king of Egypt. Remember that the Lord your God is the only God and that he is faithful. He will keep his covenant and show his constant love to a thousand generations of those who love him and obey his commands' (Deut. 7:8–9). The psalm writers constantly repeated this theme: 'O Lord, I will always sing of your constant love; I will proclaim your faithfulness for ever. I know that your love will last for all time, that your faithfulness is as permanent as the sky' (Ps. 89:1–2).

Since the word love has been so popular in discussions of Christian ethics, it has been used in many different ways. We must pay quite careful attention to the way biblical writers understood and used the word, in both Old and New Testaments. We can note four important characteristics:

1. The love of God is enduring and faithful. God's love is expressed in promises, and in a covenant, or solemn commitment. God will not turn away from his people; he does not abandon them in times of weakness or crisis.
2. God's love is forgiving. He always wants the return of his people, if they turn against him.
3. God does not choose people to love on the basis of their merit, their attractiveness, their goodness. In so far as God is ever disposed to love some people in preference to others, it is the weak, the poor, and the oppressed whom he chooses.
4. The test of true love is to be found in actions, rather than in words or feelings alone.

These four themes are fundamental, so we start with them. The nature of God's love will set the compass, and give strong substance to the foundations for detailed ethical discussion. Though the word love is not sufficient on its own to teach us morality, its main themes are indispensable for the theory of morality.

Faithful Covenant Love

God's merciful love is enduring. A favourite Hebrew word for this is '**hesed**'. Constant love, faithfulness — the nature of God's constancy is expressed in firm promises. It is also the source of God's **covenant** with his people. The Psalms especially celebrate the ever renewed and trustworthy mercy of God in a troubled and impermanent life. This is clearly a quality that can only ever be expressed imperfectly in human action. No human being is unchangeable, and therefore reliable and constant, in the way that God is. But equally clearly, human love is lacking in something if it does not share something of this quality in its own way.

It means that promises, once made, should be permanent and reliable. The upright person, says Psalm 15, 'always does what he promises, no matter how much it may cost'. If people keep their word, that certainly helps society to function more smoothly. The old saying of the London Stock Exchange 'My word is my bond', gave that institution a reputation and an efficiency which made it highly successful. But the point about promises is more than that they are socially convenient. The point is that by keeping promises, our own words reflect something of the solidity of God's word and promise. Even if, in a dishonest society, honest people stand to lose out, they should remain honest because their love of God prompts them to it.

Concern for the individual human life also owes some of its force to the covenant theme. Of course other Christian themes lead us to protect life, and for that matter to protect human rights. But the strength with which Christian ethics upholds the individual human being comes from the conviction that God himself never abandons anyone. In secular ethics, the value of the individual is often a basic assumption. The fact that this assumption is a commitment of the will and of the emotions, when it could be more solidly based, does not diminish the fundamental agreement between Christian and other ethical approaches at this point.

The outstanding example of a correspondence between moral ideals and God's covenant faithfulness is seen in **marriage**. The link here is expressed quite openly in some of the New Testament letters. 'Husbands, love your wives just as Christ loved the church and gave his life for it' (Eph. 5:21). We must recognise that patterns of married life vary a great deal in different places, and over the generations. A marriage in New Testament times clearly differed greatly from a modern marriage. There were different ways of arranging marriages, different roles in the home, different forms of intimacy, different views of responsibilities and of authority. But for all these differences, the same ideal is expressed, that a husband and wife should give themselves to one another with a degree of commitment and faithfulness modelled on the love of Christ. In a day when it is easy to long nostalgically for the days when marriage seemed much more secure, it is perhaps as well to remember the exalted nature of the ideal. If marriages are fragile today, then it is also true that being trapped in an unhappy marriage is not the ideal either. Christians differ on how to uphold the ideal in practice, and how to temper it to those for whom it feels more like a straitjacket. There need be no debate, though, about the traditional view of Christian marriage as reflecting most appropriately the faithfulness of God's covenant love in human lives.

We need to be careful at this point about trying to run the analogy the other way round, and say that God's love is just like married love. The writer of Ephesians saw the love of Christ as far above human comprehension. Making such a love the standard for ethics is much more ambitious than we usually let ourselves realise. For if we cannot fully comprehend love, then we cannot fully grasp what is right and good, much less fulfil such an ideal.[1]

Forgiving love

Forgiveness is costly. One cannot overestimate the personal strength of a man like Gordon Wilson, who forgave the IRA members

---

[1] See chapter 10 'The demand for perfection', where this is explored.

responsible for the death of his daughter. Perhaps one can overcome one's feelings of hatred in such instances, but forgiveness includes reaching out to the offender. Of course such overtures may be ignored or spurned. The forgiving love that God offers can, I think, be compared to a human parent's forgiveness of their child's killer. The death of a child is one of the most painful of bereavements. In the death of Jesus, it seems as if God himself experienced such pain.

Forgiveness is one of the ways in which we give up our own rights and interests to another. Forgiving is a way of self-giving. Many people have seen in the sacrificial death of Christ for his enemies the epitome of love. 'The greatest love a person can have for his friends is to give his life for them' (Jn. 15:13). The concern of love is always to work for the other's good, not to put oneself first. Any friendship, any marriage, any family or domestic life where people are unable to forgive and accept one another is bound to run into trouble. Putting each other first, and forgiving each other, are essential qualities of our everyday lives.

Some well-known difficulties arise here. Does forgiveness mean overlooking wrongdoing? Is there not a time for standing up for our rights? Even if we are prepared to give up our own rights, should we stand aside when the rights of others are ignored? Is it in any way practical to expect relations between groups, for instance in industry or politics, to be conducted on the basis of self-sacrifice and forgiveness? In the chapter on forgiveness, we will examine how forgiveness can be both real and realistic.

Love prefers the weak

The concern for those who are most vulnerable is a consistent biblical theme. Old Testament law is concerned for the welfare of widows, orphans, for the poor and for the stranger. This was taken up by Jesus, for instance in his parable of the judgement of the sheep and the goats. In this parable Jesus identified himself with the hungry and thirsty, the stranger, with the sick and with prisoners.

With this inspiration, Christians through the centuries have carried out countless acts of care for the needy. Traditions of medicine, education and social welfare have been created or transformed under the impact of the conviction that each person matters, no matter how insignificant or unattractive, whether or not there are claims of kinship or debt. In our own time, the world has stood in respect before the sacrificial life of Mother Teresa of Calcutta. Her concern has been with people dying in destitution. The same motivation also drives the protests of anti-abortion campaigns. But the similarity of motivation — to care for those about to be born, those about to die — is underlined by the fact that liberal abortion and euthanasia laws both endanger the lives of the defenceless.

The issues of abortion and euthanasia cannot be argued out properly at this point. I raise them to illustrate the way in which Christian viewpoints are shaped. They also illustrate another point linked with the protection of the weak, namely adherence to firm moral and legal rules. Concern to protect the vulnerable is one of the reasons for establishing firm laws. In the euthanasia debate, for instance, this is an important factor. Many fear that a liberalisation of the law, even though this is aimed at the relief of suffering, will mean that the old and sick will feel unprotected and possibly unwanted. Relaxation of the law will mean that they, their doctors and families have no choice but to consider deliberately ending their lives. The choice will explicitly be between choosing death, or allowing the dying process to run its course. The very act of raising this question at such a humanly difficult time is surely something which ought to be avoided.

Love is active

There are many different kinds of love, and many different meanings of the word. There is family love, and there is close friendship, a different kind of love. There is romantic love and sexual love; caring for a sick or handicapped child is another kind of love. One of the fundamental contrasts is between a love which desires unity with the beloved, and a love which desires the good of the one loved. In seeing where we should put the emphasis, we should begin by thinking about the love of God.

God desires unity with his people, and he also wants their welfare. Ultimately they cannot be divided, in God's final redemption from evil and suffering. Meanwhile they are related, but different. Psalm 17 sees the reward of the good man as being the presence and the sight of God: 'And I also shall see your face because my cause is just: when

I awake and see you as you are I shall be satisfied'. But the same psalm is mainly about asking for God's protection against enemies: 'Keep me as the apple of your eye: hide me under the shadow of your wings'. This verse expresses beautifully how the psalmist's prayer for God's protection belongs in a close relationship of love and trust. The assumption is that God will act to save me, because he loves me.

Jesus affirmed the same dynamic as the root of our moral lives. Because of our love for God, we live as he wishes us to. 'Whoever loves me will obey my teaching.' 'Whoever accepts my commandments and obeys them is the one who loves me'. The love of God, then, makes no division between unitive and active love. Affection and action are two aspects of the same thing.

But it does not seem that the same simplicity holds for our love of our neighbour. It is not always possible for both aspects to be so closely joined. One thinks of neighbours who cannot reciprocate the love shown, as well as those who will not. There are strangers and enemies to whom Christians still owe duties of love. The command to love still holds good when there is no way of that love being reciprocated. The love of the neighbour demands an active love, one that goes out of its way to seek his or her good.

It is possible to get the emphasis wrong here on both sides of the balance. The obvious temptation is to narrow the circle of our love, so that our love is only active towards those who also love us. The gospel is quite clear, though, that we owe love to our enemies as well as our friends. 'Why should God reward you if you only love the people who love you?' (Matt. 5:46). Concern for the poor means, too, that Christians have a duty to seek out those who are far off, and not to remain behind the walls that are so easily put up between rich and poor, between the comfortable and the struggling.

On the other hand, this cannot mean that the Christian should be equally concerned for everyone. It is important to recognise the obvious fact that we are limited beings living in a particular time and place. The duties of love that we owe to our most immediate neighbours are not identical to those owed to more distant neighbours. The point is simply that no one can be ruled out of becoming a neighbour. This does not necessarily mean that we should always give to the poor at the cost of buying life insurance for our family. On the other hand, we should not avoid giving to the poor because we have committed everything to the needs and wishes of the family.

Love for others, self-love and reason

In looking at forgiveness as one of the key aspects of Christian love, we have already seen that it is the nature of love to give itself up for others. Love sacrifices its own concerns, even its own self, for the sake of others. It is important to ask whether any other form of love, for instance one which pays attention to the needs of the self, is in some way inferior to sacrificial love. Some have maintained that any love which receives as well as gives is in some way less excellent than one which only gives.[2] But it important to notice that there is a proper kind of concern for oneself, or self-love. The command 'love your neighbour as yourself' does not legitimate all self-love, but it does not condemn it either. Not all self-love is selfishness.

In tackling this issue briefly we should first note that we are all prone to put our own interests first. So the emphasis of love is to stress that we should put the well-being of others at least on a level with our own. But when we act for the good of the other, it is hard to see why the prospect of some gain, reward or benefit for ourselves should make our action any less worthy. If I risk my life to save a friend, the fact that my friend will no doubt wish to repay me in some way if possible does not make my act a selfish one. The important point is that love should seek the welfare of the other, whether or not this necessarily involves an element of sacrifice.

Being ready to take the part of another can often require us to cross barriers, to make a mental jump over existing social divisions. Anyone is potentially a neighbour, and it can take courage to use our imagination to see someone as a neighbour who has no natural claim upon us. The needy person begging, the Bosnian refugees on the other side of Europe, the victims of poverty and famine in Africa, or of injustice in Latin America, all these are potentially our neighbours. Does true love mean that we should spontaneously respond to all their appeals whenever we come across them, at least up to what we can afford, perhaps a bit beyond? It seems hard to say no to this, but it is important

---

[2] For instance, Reinhold Niebuhr saw mutual love as inferior to altruism.

to think clearly about it. To give spontaneously to the beggar may appear loving, but it is not necessarily so. It is vital to recognise that love requires us to act wisely and rationally, as well as from our emotions. The beggar (even if genuine) may need something much more than some cash. There are issues of housing, employment, social welfare and the social fabric which may need addressing. The famine victim needs emergency help, but may also need justice and peace, as well as land or employment and the ability to provide food for the family.

To respond properly to the needy means understanding the situation of need as fully as possible. It also means making a careful judgement of the duties we owe to those who are our near neighbours, and to ourselves. Of course, we need prompting more often to care for the distant neighbour — but love does not require us to act irrationally, or to do the impossible. There are simply many needs which are not within our power to meet, many things which ought to be done which are not our responsibility.

Love and reason are not opposed. **Augustine** counted the virtue of 'prudentia', (which can be translated as prudence, or wisdom, or reason), as one of the ways in which love expresses itself. When Luther contrasted faith and love with reason and justice, he did not mean to imply that love should behave in unreasonable ways. What he did mean was that the way in which the world reasons is to be contrasted with Christian love. But this contrast can be taken too far. Love does not say that I should jump into a river to try to save a drowning child if I cannot swim. I certainly should jump if I can swim, even though there may be an element of risk and I am unlikely to be recompensed for my trouble.

Reason can be understood in different ways. That is even more true of **justice**. There are many competing views of justice. For instance, is it based on desert, or on need, or on equality? And is love to be contrasted with justice? A much more promising approach is to conceive justice as an expression of love. For instance when we think about the arrangement for taxation and social welfare, whereby money is taken from the better off to provide for those in poverty, we think in terms of justice, not love. We ask how the load of taxation can be most fairly (justly) spread, and how taxes can be as light a burden as possible. We also ask how the needs of those who are poor in a comparatively wealthy society can best be met, in a practical and positive way. Meeting their needs is also an act of justice. Different forms of justice can be seen as ways of expressing love in a way appropriate to the relationships involved. Thinking of justice in this way will not solve all the debates about justice, but it provides a helpful perspective within which these debates can be argued.

The Centrality of Christian Love

The theme of Christian love has been so central a theme in the history of theology that it is easy to take it for granted. Perhaps it is because it has been so relatively uncontroversial that it has not attracted attention in the way other doctrines have.

Augustine established the Christian doctrine of love as central and essential for his account of morality. He combined this with the Greco-Roman thought of his day about the virtues of an upright and good life. The way in which Augustine understood the phrase 'The love of God' reveals a great deal about his moral thinking. He consistently interpreted this phrase as 'The love which God shows and pours into the hearts of believers'. He took this to be the phrase's meaning even when the context makes clear that it is the believer's love of God which is intended. Augustine always wanted to emphasise the priority of God's initiative in bringing about faith, and leading the Christian to act from the love which God has given. No truly good thing is ever done, whether by the believer or unbeliever, unless it comes from love. This is not to say that good things cannot be done for other reasons, but precisely because they are done for other reasons, such as love of honour, they lack complete goodness of motive. Love is the best motive for good action, and it also determines the shape of all right conduct.

Augustine accepted the conventional scheme of the **virtues**, of which the four primary ones are justice, courage, wisdom (prudence) and self-control (temperance). These virtues express a way of life which is much richer than can be put into a single word or idea, like love. But for Augustine, all virtuous living is fundamentally a form of love in one way or another. So, the person who truly loves God will see God's righteousness, and will always act justly. So Augustine reasoned about all the virtues. It is from this perspective that we can understand Augustine's famous saying 'Love, and then do as you will'. True love is so strong that one who has received God's love and acts on that basis will always do what is right.

Aquinas followed Augustine in emphasising the centrality and primacy of love. This is sometimes overlooked because of his exposition of natural law. Aquinas' understanding of natural law was adopted by the Roman Catholic church as official church teaching. The subsequent advocacy and debates on this topic have obscured the centrality which Aquinas assigned to the doctrine of love.[3]

Luther learned much from Augustine, and he too placed love at the centre of moral thought. Luther, however, gave a new twist to ethics in contrasting love with justice. It was Luther's style to work with contrasts, opposing pairs, such as faith and reason. In such a way he contrasted love and justice. As regards the Christian's attitude to fellow Christians in the Church, love is the guide. But as far as attitudes in society are concerned, in positions of responsibility especially, our duty is to be guided by justice, in their roles as fathers, magistrates, soldiers and the like.

Many other theologians could be listed, throughout the Church's history up to the present day. We will complete our brief selection with **Karl Barth**, the greatest theologian of the twentieth century. Barth went along with the fundamental priority of love in ethics. He added to this his own special articulation of the way in which God's purposes of love belong with his work as creator. Barth uses the phrase 'covenant love' or simply 'covenant' to speak of God's redeeming love for humanity. It is covenant which expresses the centre of God's plan; the meaning of life is to be found here. Love is at the heart of things, it is the centre around which all else revolves. But if love is the centre, it is disembodied and baseless without its circumference. Creation provides the embodiment of covenant love. It is like the rim of the wheel, the circumference of the circle, with love at the centre. God created us in order to love us, and in order that we too might express

---

[3] See, for instance Paul Ramsey, *Basic Christian Ethics*, ch. VI; and Jean Porter, *The Recovery of Virtue*.

something of that love. The created order provides the basis, the pattern within which our love takes shape and reality. Barth put it like this: 'Creation is the external basis, or presupposition, of covenant; covenant is the inner meaning, the purpose of creation'. Barth's exposition of this idea proves extremely fruitful in coming to an understanding of the pattern of Christian ethics, as we will see when we look at the importance of creation for Christian ethics.

This sketch of some of the leading themes of Christian love will have to suffice. We will take them all up again in different contexts, and see more of their significance. Before we tackle the theme of creation we ought first to avoid one possible misunderstanding about the meaning of Christian covenant love. This is the sense that love is a great ideal, so long as it is not allied with restrictive or outdated doctrinal and moral tenets.

Everyday morality and Christian love

As we have already noted,[4] it is not easy to speak with great confidence about everyday morality. There are many competing outlooks, and common moral views may be somewhat vague and frequently self-contradictory. But popular morality finds it hard to find fault with the ideal of Christian love. Those who give themselves for others are praised. This contrasts with 'Christian morality', which is often dismissed as arbitrary and unreasonable. Christian morality, it is thought, makes claims for itself based on religious foundations which less and less people accept. Such a morality is often seen as restrictive and dull, appropriate only for those who voluntarily take on the yoke of Christian faith. With it comes a moral code which belongs only within that faith. So in matters of sexual and family life, in medicine, in politics and war, if Christians place themselves under their particular moral rules, that is their business. In a secular society, they have no place in pressing their views onto others who wish to be free from such arbitrary restraint.

Many Christians are also unsure about arguing the case for traditional Christian moral views. There are several hesitations. Some are not clear that an old ethic can ride the challenges of modern technological society. Others feel that life is too complex to admit of the

---

[4]   At the beginning of Chapter 1

apparent simplicities of, say, the Ten Commandments. There is a fear that Christian morality may be interpreted in obscurantist and authoritarian ways, as has happened too often in the past. And many are hesitant to argue for the truth of Christian morality in a way which may seem to condemn those of other views and beliefs.

We can respond to these hesitations by adopting Christian love as the essential foundation for ethics. Christian love is recognised by many as the highest of ideals, attractive to those within and without the Christian faith. Love does not lead to arbitrary or 'religiously-based' commands, for it is at heart rational. Love is not merely a matter of obedience to God, or of religious emotion. The way of love makes sense. It is good for us because it tries to identify the good ends for which we are created. Christian ethics aims at the good, not at restrictions and limitations. It intends to show ways in which God's good gifts can be enjoyed. Its rules and restrictions are one outworking of the love relationship between God and humanity. These rules are based on a carefully reasoned and thought out understanding of what is good for people. They attempt to protect and safeguard the good, and so they can be defended against the charge of arbitrariness.

Conclusion

In this chapter we have begun to outline the doctrine of Christian love. In future chapters we will explore some of the themes touched on here. We will examine the nature of Christian forgiveness, and try to see how forgiveness differs from mere tolerance of wrongdoing. Another theme that will return is the emphasis on love's concern for the weak and vulnerable. We will look at the powerful way in which Karl Barth expressed the relationship between covenant love and creation. 'Creation' is not just a name given to the universe, or the planet, but it is the word for the belief that God's creative purpose and action lies behind the universe. Understanding God's purposes has a vital part to play in grasping the structure of Christian ethics. First we must ask how love is to be expressed in firm rules and principles. What are the things which love will never do? Are there ways in which it will always be truly embodied?

Four

Love, Rules and Truth-Telling

The idea of morality hardly makes sense at all without moral rules.[1] There is no dispute that rules in some form or other are essential to moral thought. For instance, it cannot be right for some people to lie and cheat, while it is wrong for everyone else. Moral rules prohibiting deceit apply to everyone in much the same way. It is easy to see that if we love our neighbour, we will usually tell them the truth. Not to tell the truth means concealing something, or actively deceiving. That is no way to show our love. It lacks respect and concern for them, for their right to the truth, and for our relationship with them.

But does love mean that we should simply obey the rule 'Always tell the truth'? There appear to be at least two serious reasons not to accept this. In the first place, we experience occasions when the most loving thing to do seems to be not to tell the truth. Perhaps this means just by remaining silent, but sometimes it may seem more loving actually to tell a lie. On such occasions the rule seems to get in the way of love, not to express love. The fact that love comes first must make us very cautious about insisting on other definite rules.

In the second place, there seems something odd about saying that love can be translated into rules. Is there not a huge difference between responding to our neighbours out of love, and following a set of rules which tell us how we should treat them? Indeed, someone who simply acts in mechanical obedience to a set of rules can hardly be thought

---

[1] By 'rules' here we mean any kind of general moral command or statement, including laws and moral principles. A distinction is usually made between principles, laws and rules. More general moral sayings are called principles, such as 'Love your neighbour' and 'Murder is always wrong'. More specific commands such as 'Feed your children' are known as rules, while the contents of legislation are called 'laws'. Here we are using the word 'rule' for all kinds of moral sayings.

of as acting morally at all. Surely the essence of love is that it alone should control the motives for our behaviour.

These are no doubt two of the concerns which have led us to shift the language of morals away from moral rules, and to speak of values instead. For values appear to speak of flexibility and the sense of whole-hearted allegiance which we are looking for. So, in advocating the necessity of rules in our moral understanding, we must remain aware of these two concerns. The point, however, is not whether we prefer one language of morality to another, but which language best helps us to understand the meaning of morality.

In seeing whether love can be embodied in definite moral rules, we will take as our example the issue of truth-telling.

The Rule of Truth-telling

If we love our neighbour, will we always tell the truth? Is the rule of truth-telling altogether without exceptions? Even if we are rigorously committed to truth, we recognise times for keeping silence. There are, after all, confidential matters which should not be told. Or to take another example, in telling a story, we do not simply tell the truth.

Neither of these examples involves actually telling an untruth to deceive someone. But there are occasions when some form of lie may well be considered morally appropriate. We can think of: (a) the polite lie, told in order to reassure and encourage, to show friendliness; (b) the protective lie, told in order to shield someone from bad news which they are not in a position to receive; and (c) the lie told to protect the innocent by deceiving an unjust aggressor. Let us give some examples of each of these situations:

a) The polite lie

There are occasions when we are only slightly acquainted with someone, when our concern is to establish our genuine goodwill towards them. If we are staying in someone else's home, the natural reply to 'Did you sleep well?' is 'Very well, thank you.' This would be a natural and polite response even if we had lain awake most of the night, perhaps worrying about a problem, or perhaps unaccustomed to such a firm mattress or the quality of night silence in the countryside. Perhaps we could avoid the question with 'I was very comfortable, thank you.' But even if we could think of an accurate way of answering, supposing that the bed we had used was really very old and uncomfortable, and the room very cold, it would be by no means easy to combine polite reassurance and gratitude and at the same time tell our hosts the important truth that their spare room actually needed some attention! It might well be right to conceal that fact from them, and hope they would find it out from someone else.

b) The protective lie

The classic instance of the felt need for the protective lie is in caring for the very ill. Perhaps there is bad news to tell about a close member of the family, or perhaps it is the truth about the patient's own illness. If a patient, in the early stages of a terminal illness but not yet knowing that, asks for reassurance, most doctors have as their immediate concern to reassure the patient even if their longer term concern is to help the patient know and accept the truth of their condition. On most occasions, of course, such questions can be deflected or avoided without inaccuracy until the doctor is confident that the patient is ready to hear the whole diagnosis. But such deflection is a form of withholding the truth, even if lying is not actually involved. As such, there may be a mild form of deception involved. If so, it certainly seems as if love's concern for the sick person goes against the principle of truth-telling.

c) Lies told to an enemy

Actual lying is certainly involved in our third example. Moralists have debated whether we should tell a lie to deceive a would-be murderer, when we are hiding the potential victim. Love for the victim surely demands that we should protect him, by lying to his attacker if necessary. A well-known example occurred in World War II, when Jews were protected from the Nazi SS seeking them out for sending to concentration camps. Corrie ten Boom, in a devout Christian family in occupied Holland, tells how they felt they had to lie in such circumstances. More generally, the protection of intelligence sources, in times of peace and war, can involve elaborate games of deceit. Anyone who accepts the need for national security, and the maintenance of armed forces to protect it, must I think accept that lies must sometimes be told in that cause. There is of course biblical precedent for such lying. Rahab is known as the woman who shielded Israelite spies in Jericho, deceiving her own people to protect the spies. Since she was also commended in the New Testament it is good evidence that lying may sometimes be acceptable in times of hostility.

These examples all remind us that the task of truth telling involves balancing respect for the truth with speech appropriate to the relationships concerned. For the most part there is no problem since telling the truth serves to build trust and relationships. But, to take the third example first, the kind of relationship we have with an enemy means that we do not owe him the truth of our plans. Mostly, we keep secrets not by lying, but by security precautions of other kinds. But this cannot prevent occasions arising when a lie is the only way to protect a secret. This is not to say that all our knowledge is rightly concealed from an enemy. Both convention and humanity require, for instance, that we should pass on basic information about prisoners of war.

In the second example, of answering the questions of a sick patient, there can be no question that the truth of their condition belongs to the patient, not to the medical staff alone. But concern for the patient makes clear that the truth is theirs to know, and theirs not to know as well. There are those who would rather remain in ignorance of the truth; some patients deny knowledge of their diagnosis after having been told it. It is no part of medical care to insist that patients know the truth, though it may well be beneficial for them to know it and come to terms with it. The medical task is then to impart the truth at the right place and the right time, when the patient genuinely asks for it and thereby exercises their undoubted right to it.

In the first example, there are two possibly conflicting truths to be told. The guest wishes to convey the truth that he is grateful and well-disposed to his hosts, but he is also asked for the truth about whether he slept well. The adept person will perhaps find a way of combining both in the answer he gives. But it is the first message which will often take priority, that of reassuring the hosts and thus expressing gratitude and goodwill. If I lay awake out of worry, or simply because I only sleep well in my own bed, then that is not something that my hosts need to know.

Paul Ramsey suggested that the rule of truth-telling should be expressed as 'Never withhold the truth from one to whom it is due'.[2] This formulation seems to catch accurately the points we have looked at. Truth is not due to the enemy, it is due to the patient in a certain way and at the right time, and maybe only some of the truth is due to the host. Usually, truth should be told. 'Never withhold the truth' expresses the imperative of respect for the truth, and it also covers the point that there may be other forms of deceit than simply lying. The phrase 'From one to whom it is due' catches accurately the cases when the nature of the relationships mean that truth should not be told in full. The reason that this phrase is helpful is because it accurately catches the question that should be asked. It locates the question that has to be asked, namely 'What is the truth that is due to this person?' This question then has to be answered (the presumption being of course that the truth is normally due).

Ramsey's statement of the rule works well because it rests on an understanding of the issues that are involved. This is why it is to be preferred to another suggestion 'Never tell a lie, except when life can be saved by doing so'. This appears to cover our second and third examples (especially the third, that of lying in wartime). But it is not quite accurate. It is certainly not right to tell a lie to save a guilty man from punishment. Nor does it help with the first example, the polite lie, or other instances we might think of. For instance, should we ever tell a lie to protect a confidential secret? The command 'Never tell a lie, except . . .' will need a good deal of careful drafting to meet the instances we can think of, and even then is unlikely to be complete. On the other hand, Ramsey's version leaves open to us the task of interpretation in exactly the right area. It points us in the right direction in considering new instances. So, for instance, it covers the question of confidentiality in exactly the right way. The confessor and the counsellor are right to protect their confidential secrets. Clearly they normally do this by simply refusing to say anything. But it is not hard to visualise

---

[2] 'The Case of the Curious Exception', in *Norm and Context in Christian Ethics*, p. 89.

circumstances when a lie might actually be necessary to protect such a secret.

This approach to the rule of truth-telling gives us important pointers as we try to work out what it exactly it means to insist on strong moral rules which are neither too rigid to be accurate nor too open to exceptions to be of any real help. We have seen that it is possible to understand the moral rule against lying in a way that does justice to the relevant considerations. This makes it possible to formulate the moral rule flexibly, but also specifically enough to apply quite directly. It is not too general to give practical help, as the general principle 'Respect the truth' is. Nor is it too rigid and specific, as when we say 'Always tell the whole truth to whoever asks for it', to do justice to every occasion. In saying 'Never withhold the truth from one to whom it is due', we are clear that on the vast majority of occasions, this simply means 'Do not withhold the truth'. But it allows for those times when someone is not entitled to know everything that we know.

It is important to emphasise that other moral areas need to be examined in a similar way. For instance, 'respect for life' is also capable of clear expression in specific moral rules. It is true that Christians differ about exactly what those rules should be (just as they do over the question of truth-telling). One view is that no Christian should ever take the life of another, for any reason, even in war or capital punishment. Others argue that life may have to be taken in order to protect the lives of other, innocent, people. An argument such as this does not invalidate the rules. On the contrary, the debate is an important one, and it is best conducted by seeing which rules most express our understanding of the substantial issue. Similar discussions are also vital in the areas of property, marriage, and so on.

When Moral Rules Conflict

Situations can arise in which different rules prescribe contradictory courses of action. Sometimes it seems that it is best to conceal the truth, or actively lie, out of love for someone. Perhaps the pursuit of justice may lead us to break the law, when the law itself is ineffective. We may get involved in a conflict of loyalties, when we have to deceive one person in order to protect another. O'Donovan gives the following example.[3] A good friend of yours admits that he is deeply involved with a mistress behind his wife's back. His wife is also a friend. Is it our duty to warn her? Is our loyalty to him or to her? Is our loyalty to the truth, or to the institution of marriage? If nothing is said, is it perhaps more likely that he will give up the affair and his marriage survive? In instances like this, we need to admit that human lives are too complex for simple resolution. No moral rule can do more than give pointers, or strong suggestions.

Some have suggested that we need a hierarchy of duties. So we might say that saving life is more important than telling the truth, and that telling the truth is more important than protecting property. But no simple hierarchy of this kind seems likely to be able to cover all possibilities. We might very well think that truth might be more important than life. It would not be right, for instance, to tell a lie in court, giving a false alibi to save a guilty person from capital punishment. Nor would it be right to tell such a lie even to save an innocent person from an unjust conviction. Such examples could easily be multiplied. Alternatively, it may be suggested that our duty is to weigh the greater and lesser evils. The problem with this approach is that if it is carried too far, it effectively means dissolving all our moral rules in favour of saying 'Always do that which leads to the greatest good and the least evil'. If we are to retain some moral rules in our approach, we will need some clear sense of when an attempt to choose the lesser evil is appropriate.

Another suggestion is that on some occasions there is no escape from doing something wrong. We should simply admit this, and not try to insist that there is some 'right' course of action. Sometimes it also helps to recognise that owing to the wrongdoing of others, we can be forced into a position from which there is no escape without some wrong. Perhaps we might share some of the blame, or perhaps we are quite innocent. Either way, we must break some moral rule. This would mean that moral compromise is inevitable from time to time. There may be some truth in this, but it does not help us to decide what we should actually do. Nor is it helpful to talk too freely of moral

---

[3] *Resurrection and Moral Order*, pp. 198–9.

compromise, for there is more than one kind of compromise. Many compromises are simply euphemisms for doing something wrong, when the right thing would have been perfectly possible, even if costly.

When rules say the wrong thing

Another difficulty is that moral rules may sometimes appear to prescribe the wrong thing. For instance, when filling one's car at a self-service petrol station, it is a form of theft to drive off without paying. But suppose one is on an urgent dash to hospital, without money, or time to explain the emergency to the attendant. Surely it would be the right thing to take the necessary petrol, in order to get to hospital to save the sick person? Is this contravening the moral rule against theft? When I put this to a friend who happens to be a solicitor, he quickly pointed out that there would be no theft if one returned at the earliest opportunity to pay for the petrol.[4] To think otherwise is to misunderstand the law of theft, for on this occasion there was no intention to withhold payment. As it happens in this case, the moral rule against theft appears to be virtually identical with English law. Any moral rule needs to be understood intelligently (and the same also applies to the law, of course!). In this instance, we need to formulate the rule against theft with care, just as we did with the rule against lying.

Applying moral rules

The usefulness of fixed rules also seems to be diminished by the recognition that there are many areas for which there can be no simple rules. There is a duty laid on those who have plenty to be generous and to use some of their wealth to help provide for the needy. But how generous is generous? Is generosity to be measured in the size of the donation? A large donation from someone living on a state pension would be a trifling sum if given by a wealthy lawyer. Thought also needs to go into the generous act. Is it hardness of heart or good commonsense to turn one's back on the alcoholic begging in the high street? Such encounters need to be tackled with the gentleness of doves

---

[4] In English law, at any rate.

but the cunning of serpents![5] Many everyday political choices are questions of a shrewd preference of this kind. There is, for instance, a moral dimension to fixing the level of welfare benefits, but there is certainly no easy moral calculus. It cannot simply be said that it is always morally right to raise unemployment benefit. One must bear many other things in mind, such as the maintenance of incentives to find work, competing calls for expenditure, and other priorities. Here are all kinds of choices with a moral dimension, but discerning our moral duty cannot be done with precision. Much less can a moral code prescribe the right course of action under all circumstances.

A further challenge to traditional moral formulations is posed by the continual emergence of new technology. The last half-century has seen the discovery of nuclear power, and the last fifteen years have seen many medical advances. Those which concern the beginnings and endings of human lives pose many new moral questions. Clearly it is not possible simply to give answers to such questions purely by a simple extrapolation from existing moral rules. The existence of such new questions also makes us wary of fixed moral certainties. For such is the pace of change that we cannot be sure that new questions will not arise in quite unforeseen areas.

Considerations like this remind us that there is much more to moral understanding than mere rules. In arguing that there are some ways in which love will always behave — or never behave — we must not think that these will cover everything. It is important to be able to say with confidence that we should never deceive an innocent person, nor commit wanton violence, nor live a carelessly promiscuous sex life. These are a few minimal prohibitions. Positively, it is good to be generous, caring, trustworthy, thoughtful. Love will always express itself in such ways. But we cannot easily tie down and define what care, thoughtfulness and generosity will actually and precisely consist of. The expression of Christian love will be shaped in accordance with the realities of life.

There are, then, some clear and definite moral rules. But there is another objection to any reliance on moral rules. Some point out that unless our decisions and actions spring from the heart, they can hardly claim to be truly moral.

---

[5] cf. Martin Luther King, *Strength to Love*.

Morality is a Matter of the Heart

The ethics of love is part of the mainstream of Christian tradition in arguing for the importance of moral rules. Roman Catholic teaching, as well as conservative Protestant outlook, is agreed on this. However, there are several important difficulties with seeing morality as essentially governed by a code of rules. We can provisionally divide the difficulties into two sorts. One sort of objection to rules points out that moral action is much more than obedience to a code. Truly good moral behaviour is a matter of action freely and willingly undertaken, it is something chosen rather than enforced. True goodness is a matter of the heart and mind, it cannot be merely mechanical, like simply following a set of instructions.

An old Protestant concern, stemming especially from Luther, is that the Christian has no need of laws and rules for moral guidance.[6] Instead, the Christian will naturally act out of love. Responding to the free grace of God, the Christian is transformed by the **Holy Spirit** and is led to do the right thing. This is not behaviour which is governed by rules. Indeed, a concern for moral rules can lead Christians to try to earn their own righteousness, and fall back into an attempt to gain their own salvation through their own effort, rather than by the free justification offered to those who have faith in Christ.

This objection confuses the motivation and the method of Christian living with the actual pattern and substance of Christian love. Our concern with moral rules is to describe the ways in which love will always act. It is not that the Christian's most profound reasons for acting in certain ways are because the rules say so. The basic motivation, as the Protestant rightly says, is to live a life which responds to God's love, and as far as possible embodies or reflects that love. In hard cases, it is not appropriate or possible to consult some kind of moral handbook which will prescribe the right course of action. Human life is in any case too complex and varied for that. The rules play their part in the process of discernment. If we accept the rule 'Never withhold the truth from one to whom it is due', then we may still have to think hard about who the truth belongs to. Careful thought

---

[6] See for instance Luther's 'The Freedom of a Christian', in e.g., *Martin Luther: Selections from his writings*, John Dillenberger (ed.).

and reasoning are called for, to try to see what the morally relevant features of the situation are. It is here that the work of clarifying moral rules, their meaning and application, will be of great help in alerting us to the relevant features and circumstances.

There is a more general form of this objection. The Protestant objection sees behaviour motivated by rules as not springing from the heart, from the love of God for every believer. Any behaviour which is morally worthy must be that which the person genuinely identifies with and wants to do. There is credit, for instance, in repaying a debt even when one is forced to, for which one will suffer if the debt is not repaid. But a truer test of goodness lies in repaying a debt which the borrower has completely forgotten, when one could easily get away with not paying. It is one thing to repay a mortgage, but there is more credit in making a full and honest declaration of income tax liability when it would be easy enough to conceal some taxable income. The first is simply a matter of commonsense. One will get into trouble if the mortgage is not repaid, possibly losing the house. But to pay tax when it could easily enough be evaded shows someone whose heart is turned towards honesty, toward contributing a fair share to the nation's needs. This is something quite different from following the tax laws only because one knows one will otherwise be found out. This characteristically Protestant objection to rules does not see someone governed by rules as a good person, just someone who is rather dull, unadventurous and respectable.

Again, this objection fails to recognise the distinction between motivation and action, between the subjective and the objective. The good person pays tax with a degree of willingness, seeing the reason for taxes, while nobody can take moral credit for paying tax merely because they are forced to. But these different motivations are nothing to do with what is actually owed in tax. Both the person who pays tax grudgingly and the one who pays it willingly still have to work out their tax obligations. The tax laws specify what is due from each. One pays the legal amount, concealing nothing, while the other looks for ways not to pay, legally or illegally. But both need to know what is due. A similar argument applies to our moral obligations. Even when we are entirely concerned to serve our neighbour, we need to know what that entails. Of course that does not mean consulting a literal or mental codebook, but it does mean understanding our neighbour's needs, and seeing how best to serve them. This does not mean that every detail is covered by rules. But it certainly does allow for some prohibitions, and also for some positive rules of general applicability.

It is essential to distinguish motivation from substance. We are not concerned to clarify moral rules in order to condemn others who break them, nor in order that we may rely on them alone in our moral life. We are not to think that in understanding and keeping a set of moral rules we are thereby justified, or morally good. The point of the technical discussions of how rules work is that it will help us understand more about moral truth. It will help us see how our knowledge of God's creation purposes and his covenant love can be embodied in some of the difficult areas of moral decision. Our aim in our discussion is also to show that we can have reasonable confidence in moral rules as giving clear and reliable guidance on the matters they concern.

Rules and Popular Morality

We have seen that a morality based on Christian love will be happy with some definite moral rules. Such rules may be flexible, in that the concern to express love remains the basic aim. And obedience to rules is not in contradiction with acting out of genuine, heartfelt moral conviction. It is clear that these insights can be quite easily transposed into other moral approaches. For instance, one who sees moral motivation as concern for the welfare of others, or for the greatest human good, could derive moral rules in a very similar way.

It is usually supposed that if rules have exceptions, then the rules are less useful, less to be trusted. If there are exceptions then the rule is weakened. If there are times when we should withhold the truth, does that not weaken our concern for truth at all times? The existence of hard cases and painful dilemmas seems to bring the whole idea of true moral rules into question. There seems to be little doubt that many moral rules are under threat in everyday life, though it is also quite easy to exaggerate this. There is a perverse comfort to be found in bemoaning how bad things have got! Fascination with moral dilemmas has a lot to do with the status of moral rules. In challenging traditional rules, or showing that they do not always 'work', there is often an implicit threat to moral motivation in general.

We cannot accept this apparently obvious conclusion. The fact is that defining rules with care strengthens them, it does not weaken them. When we see why and in what circumstances it may not be right to give the whole truth, we are under even firmer obligation to tell the whole truth on the occasions when that is what is demanded. If we recognise the exceptions accurately, and carefully, then we define and strengthen the rule. The doctor who withholds a diagnosis for a time does so out of respect and care for the patient. But that same care and respect teaches that the truth ultimately belong to the patient, and may not be withheld indefinitely. Moral rules can really make good sense. They are not fixed, rigid and arbitrary.

Nor is it hard to see that obedience to rules can quite well go along with genuine personal conviction. The point is that we obey the rules because they embody the nature of love. They remind us of our obligations of love. Married people do not remain married purely because of marriage law. But the law nevertheless defines some of their marriage commitment, and may help them to fulfil it when love itself grows cold for a time. The marriage law embodies love's ideal, or part of it. But someone who marries purely to satisfy the law has missed the point. Legalism is not enough. But in challenging rigid and legalistic ideas of morality, our culture has often done much to undermine moral conviction itself.

The connection between motivation and moral rules can also be put the other way round. If moral rules are necessary, they are certainly not sufficient. They are not the whole of morality. Without a firm foundation, moral rules are little more than an arbitrary legalism. Those who wish to see our moral culture renewed need to give thought to moral foundations as well as to rules and principles. Moral theologians have frequently claimed that it is hard to find good secular foundations for moral belief. Our civilisation owes more to Christianity than it is presently prepared to admit. Ideas of concern for human welfare, or of human rights, or of the greatest human good are historical derivatives of Christian convictions. Many have feared that when Christian faith dwindled, moral beliefs would inevitably dwindle also.

Love is the most fundamental element of Christian morality. But it is not the only aspect of Christian faith that we need. In giving fuller answers to the radical questions now being asked of moral traditions, we need in particular to resort to the belief that God made the world. In creation, God gave both order and purpose to the world that he made.

Five

The Importance of Creation

Love provides the driving force for morality. The good human life is one which is shaped by the aim of reflecting God's love. Such love forms the basis for the difference between right and wrong, and gives content to that difference. Not only our actions, but our thoughts and inmost selves, are claimed by love. The claim of morality reaches our intentions and desires, not merely the things we do and say. We have also seen that the consistency of love means that there are clear moral rules covering different areas of life.

Love takes its shape in relation to the realities of life. Love needs to be expressed intelligently, and in a way that is in touch with everyday realities. It is easy to see that love means respect for life, for truth, for property and so on. But love alone does not tell us in detail what to do at the edges of life, for instance. What does love mean for the one who is dying? Or for those just about to begin their life? To be able to understand the meaning of love, we need also to consider the doctrine of **creation**.

The word 'creation' is very often associated with the ideas of beauty and wonder. When Christians meet on a sunny spring morning they will often praise God for his creation, for the sunshine, spring flowers, for freshness and beauty. The words of the Victorian hymn 'Morning has broken' express the popular sentiment well: 'Fresh the first dewfall, sunlit from heaven' — 'God's recreation of the new day'. The word creation is understood to mean nature — trees, grass, spring flowers, rain and sun.

As often as not, this theme provokes another thought. Modern human activity is so powerful, and moving so fast, that creation itself seems under threat. The harnessing of natural energy in large machinery, and its systematic organisation, is something genuinely new, and on a scale large enough to alter the 'nature' of the planet in ways unprecedented for millions of years. The image, in contrast to a sunny spring morning, is of a mechanical digger tearing up the landscape, or perhaps of a factory pouring its waste products into the atmosphere and into a nearby river. Much concern is expressed that if some of these activities are unchecked, they will render the earth less and less habitable by human beings, and many other life-forms. Concerns range from the heating up of the whole planet (the 'greenhouse'-effect), through the large scale destruction of rainforests, to the threats to individual species, from whales to butterflies. So the fear is expressed that we are destroying God's good creation.

The word 'creation' is often used as if it meant exactly the same as the word 'nature'. For the most part, to say 'nature is beautiful' or 'nature is at risk' would express what we mean more accurately. For the word 'creation' points to a more fundamental Christian truth. When we say, with the opening words of the Bible 'In the beginning God created the universe', we are saying more than simply that we discern God's hand behind our existence. In causing us to exist God gave the universe pattern and shape, form and beauty. More than this, he created it with specific purposes and intentions. In the account given by Genesis, the birds and creatures are given the responsibility of reproducing, to increase and to fill the earth. The plants, grass and fruit and so on, are given to humankind and to the animals as food — that is how their purpose is seen. Human beings are given very special responsibilities, including bringing the earth under control.

So, to believe in God as creator has radical and far-reaching implications, alongside other tenets of Christian faith. It is a belief, in the same sense as the love of God, or the coming of Jesus Christ as the Son of God, are beliefs of the Christian faith. These beliefs provide anchors for our life, and they have potential to affect everything about the way we think and the way we live.

The Importance of the Belief in Creation for Christian Ethics

The belief that God has created the world has vital implications for all our ethics, not just for our use of the natural world. It affects our view of marriage, of medicine, of justice, of truth, as well as of ecology and technology. We can summarise some of the most important implications in a few propositions.

1.   The order in creation means that we should expect to find continuities and regularities in our lives. One human being is recognisably like another in some fundamental ways. We are each entitled to respect, to justice, to truth, in certain critical ways. Similarly, one marriage is like another, though of course no two are identical (just as no two human beings are identical). Recognising these continuities, in the midst of all our variety, is essential. For some continuities mean that the moral demands made on us are essentially similar — to be faithful to our marriage partners, to tell the truth, to respect life. This may seem obvious, but it gives a basis for moral rules and principles. In the modern world where humanity has new power to reshape the world, this task of recognising God's intended patterns becomes ever more essential.

     This point could also be put negatively. For without order in the world, there would be no moral categories, and all moral speech would effectively be meaningless. If every person and every situation was wholly different and unique, without any similarities, then moral demands would also be variable and unpredictable. We would only be able to talk about morality in the most general terms, as perhaps 'Always try to do good'. Even that assumes that we know something about what is good.

2.   Part of the created pattern is that things and people have purposes intended by the creator. This proposition runs strongly against a modern scientific assumption. Science makes the assumption that there are no inbuilt purposes, which is a necessary assumption for scientific reasons. Increasingly, this assumption has worked its way into many other areas of life. But for Christian aspects of life, it is important to recognise that there are intrinsic, inbuilt, purposes in the world. We are not free to invent our own

purposes in every respect. Perhaps most crucially, we are not free to invent purposes for other people. Other people, that is to say, should be treated as 'ends' in themselves, not as means to our ends, to our purposes. But there are inbuilt purposes in other features of life too, such as marriage, or speech, or private property. These purposes, which have to be carefully discerned, are given. They are not invented, and so not open to wholesale reinvention.

3. Creation is varied, and in many ways open-ended. The first two propositions alone might seem to imply that all our lives can be governed by moral rules derived from understanding God's plans for us. But the creation is both patterned and varied. One leaf may be like another, and one tree like another, as far as their basic biology goes, but this is far from saying that they are identical. Human lives are even more infinitely varied. Moral tensions and conflicts are to be expected from time to time, because there are many different patterns and therefore moral claims, that impinge on our lives. Not only so, but there is genuine freedom, and open-endedness, in human life. There are many different ways of speaking the truth, for instance, not just one.

4. The order within creation sometimes imposes limits on our moral freedom. There are things which we ought to do, and things which we ought not to do, if we are to respect God's ordering of creation. We readily recognise limits in the way we know that we should treat one another. What also needs to be wisely discerned is where there are limits even to what people freely consent to do together. There are also, no doubt, moral limits to technological invention and change.

5. The creation is God's gift to us, and we should learn to value it rightly. The gift is not the same as the giver. Creation is not the source of value; it does not provide the ultimates on which we should build our lives. But the creation is good, and should be affirmed and enjoyed in the way it is given to us.

So the doctrine of creation is an essential foundation for ethics. If we are to know the structures of morality, the way in which our moral lives should be ordered, then we need to understand God's purposes for different aspects of the world. For instance, to know why marriage is good requires some understanding of the point of gender, of sexuality, of parenthood and so on. This is not to say that nature dictates what should be done, in the sense that we should only do what is 'natural'. It is right, for instance, to cultivate the fields, to grow plants and fruits in an ordered way, not just to let them grow as they will and then forage for them. In one sense, after all, cultivation is not natural, it is an ordered human activity. The human responsibility is to discern God's purposes for creation, which may or may not be relatively straightforward. All we can say is that the progress of technology of all kinds is throwing up questions for this kind of discernment with great rapidity. Does God intend that we should harness nuclear energy, that we should fertilise human beings in vitro, or that we should deliberately engineer new plants (such as new strains of wheat, etc.)? There are no easy answers to these questions in the doctrine of creation. But it does give a particular perspective within which to approach them.

Creation: a brief Biblical Survey

The first chapter of Genesis has become an unfortunate battle ground between those who insist on a literal reading and the majority who have preferred the modern scientific history of the universe and the evolutionary theory of life on earth. Sadly, this has obscured the fact that if the chapter is read as a 'poetic' interpretation of God's creation, it has a very clear outlook which remains highly relevant. Two points are usually noted, but very often they remain the limits of theological comment. The goodness of God's work is clear. The refrain 'And God saw that it was good' runs through the chapter. The attention to the creation of human beings is also usually noted. God gives human beings responsibility, putting them in charge of the earth, the animals and birds. Human beings are the summit of God's activity, and they are made in God's image. These are the themes that have largely claimed the attention of commentators and theologians.

In the light of the new questions being asked today, we need to learn more about the Bible's thought about creation. For instance, there is an air of calm reason, of an ordered patterning. God creates by his word, he makes separations and distinctions. Clearly we cannot agree with all the actual separations of which the writer speaks, like the separation of the water in the heavens from the water on earth. The separation of light from darkness on day one reads oddly to us, especially when we find that the sun and the moon were not made until day four. But I do not think this should obscure the point which I suppose we largely take for granted – that the universe is a highly ordered structure. For the writer of Genesis this order exists by the word and action of God.

We should also note that there are many purposes, some clearly stated, and some only implied, in the story of creation. The separation of earth from sea makes possible the growth of plants on earth, and gives a place for fish and for animals. More explicitly, purposes are assigned to many things created on the fourth, fifth and sixth days. The heavenly bodies are meant to mark the regularly changing seasons. The sun and moon are given for day and night, to separate light from darkness. The purposes given to living creatures are that they should reproduce and fill the earth. We have already noted the intention of God for humanity, that people should subdue the earth.

The order and purposes given by God are evidence that there are limits to human dominion, ordering and reordering of the world. But this could give a misleading picture if we did not also recognise that God clearly gives real responsibility and autonomy to his creation. On one level this is as simple as noticing that it is not God himself who fills the earth with plants, fish and animals. Instead, he gives to living creatures the ability to bear seed and to reproduce. The creation of more living beings comes about independently of God's immediate directions. What is true of plants and animals is much more true of human beings. Humankind is given genuine responsibility and freedom in the task of caring for the earth.

This is an important theme, for it is emphasised in dramatic terms in the next chapter. In the second Genesis story of creation, man is created first, not last, and then the animals, and finally woman. It is man (we should not read anachronistic sexist points into this) who is given the job of naming the animals. This is an emphatic way of saying that people are genuinely left in charge, for if God were to keep direct control he would surely have named the animals. Instead he withdraws into the background.

The theme of creation is not often dwelt on in the rest of the scriptures, though it is clearly an important assumption, for example in Isaiah (see ch 40 for instance). The New Testament takes the sovereignty of God in creation as absolutely fundamental (e.g., Matt. 19:4; Jn. 1; Rom. 8:18–22; Col 1: 15–20). But it is the Wisdom literature which most gives space to dwelling on the nature of God's work in creation. Many psalms praise God for the goodness of what he has made, and for his generous provision for men and women. Here is a short excerpt (Ps. 104:14–17):

> You water the mountains from your dwelling on high:
> and the earth is filled by the fruits of your work.
> You cause the grass to grow for the cattle:
> and all green things for the servants of mankind.
> You bring food out of the earth:
> and wine that makes glad the heart of man,
> oil to give him a shining countenance:
> and bread to strengthen his heart.

Proverbs ch 8 celebrates God's wisdom in the work of creation — in a famous personification wisdom is God's first creation, and is beside him as his architect, taking pleasure as good things come into being. The theme of wisdom is also instructively developed in the book of Job. In chapter 28 human initiative and ingenuity is fully acknowledged. Not even the lion, nor the farseeing hawk, has any inkling of men's activity in mining silver, gold, iron and precious stones from the depths of the earth.

> Men dig the hardest rocks,
> Dig mountains away at their base.
> As they tunnel through the rocks,
> They discover precious stones.
> They dig to the sources of rivers
> And bring to light what is hidden.
> But where can wisdom be found?
> Where can we learn to understand?   (Job 28:9–12)

The last couplet brings us a sharp surprise, with its opening 'But'. Human beings may be clever, highly ingenious, but this is not the same as wisdom. In fact:

> Wisdom is not to be found among men;
> No one knows its true value.
> The depths of the oceans and seas
> Say that wisdom is not found there.
> It cannot be bought with silver or gold   (Job 28:13–15).

The same pessimistic view of human knowledge is even more powerfully expressed in the overwhelming concluding chapters of the book:

> Then out of the storm the LORD spoke to Job. 'Who are you to question my wisdom with your ignorant empty words? Stand up now like a man and answer the questions I ask you. Were you there when I made the world? If you know so much, tell me about it'   (Job 38:1–4).

Even when we have made the necessary allowances for the pervasive pessimism of the book of Job, we must acknowledge that the theme expressed so one-sidedly here is still an authentic biblical insight. For all biblical writers from Genesis to Revelation, there is an irreducible gulf between the creative power, the sovereignty of God, and the limited ability and responsibility of human beings. The human race has dignity, greatness and glory, but this is certainly not directly comparable with the greatness of God himself, (see for example Ps. 8). To find wisdom, men and women must seek it in humility from God. It is not automatic, but rather it has to be learned.

Let us summarise some of the important themes of Genesis and the biblical tradition concerning the nature of creation. First, creation is good. It is the generous gift of God, who makes happiness and fulfilment possible in rich diversity. Second, creation is ordered. It will follow from this that an important human task is to discern possibilities within that order. Partly this makes scientific knowledge possible. But more, it means that the good human life will also find its best possibilities in obedience to that order, not by challenging it in the wrong way. Thirdly, the patterns of God's creation are significantly understood in terms of the purposes they serve. It is in the light of these purposes that we can discern what we should aim at in our

technological transformation of the world. Fourthly, the real autonomy and independence given by God means that there is real work
for humankind. Whether or not it is right to mine the earth for
minerals, to split the atom, to perform blood transfusions, to invent
antibiotics or to undertake research into aging — these are genuine
questions for the human race. God, we may say, does not prescribe
or prevent such possibilities, for they are matters of real human choice
and decision. Finding the right and wrong of such knowledge and
technology is not something which can simply be read off from
revelation, or 'the way things are'. Fifthly, then, humanity has the
privilege and the task of dominion over the earth. We will have to
answer for the way in which this gift has been used, but it is not a gift
which can be given up or, as it were, buried in the ground! Sixthly,
the most difficult task in interpreting and using creation is in finding
wisdom, to set the direction of our lives rightly. It is one thing to build
and sail a seaworthy vessel, another to navigate it accurately. Without
accurate navigation all our fine shipbuilding technology, while in
many ways admirable, is ultimately worthless.

Order and Pattern in Creation

The ordered structures, patterns and continuities of God's creation are
an important element of its goodness. As we have already seen, order
provides a basis for morality itself. But there is more to be said here.
The goodness of creation is often undervalued by the common
reaction against discipline. There is a feeling that anything truly good
is in some way inevitable, spontaneous or unusual. Such is the
impression very often given by great sportsmen and women, by great
artists, by orators or teachers. Any really good achievement in such
human activities will usually give an appearance of fluency and
'naturalness' which conceals the effort and discipline which has gone
into the preparation. Of course, without the structured discipline,
without careful thought and experiment, there could be no genuine
fluency and success. Behind the apparent goodness of creation and
human moral living lies a strong structure. This structure is given, and
needs to be recognised, not invented.

Some allege that the emphasis on order and discipline can be negative, and result in obscuring our enjoyment of the goodness that is given to us. There is no doubt that this has sometimes been an element in traditional teaching. There is a story about a church minister whose house lay opposite the church on the other side of a lake. The lake froze one winter, and the minister skated over the lake to take the Sunday worship. Some church members took offence at this, feeling that the law of Sunday observance had been breached by the minister's unusual way of getting to church. They took their complaint to the church council. After careful consideration, the council pronounced that it was acceptable for the minister to skate to church, provided that he derived no pleasure from doing so!

This negative outlook is not at all what is meant by true discipline. But there is a danger that emphasising moral limits can lead us to undervalue the goodness of God's gifts. Some critics of covenant ethics fear this above all. Advocates of creation spirituality emphasise that human feelings and reactions are part of God's good creation. The task of morality is seen as pointing us to the possibilities for harmony, for enjoying good things, not in erecting barriers to positive discovery of the world's and our own goodness. Their concern is with freedom, with emotions not restrictive reasoning. On the other hand, those who stress human responsibility lay great emphasis on reason, rather than emotion. Their problem with given patterns of morality is that they see the task as that of reshaping the world, not with accepting it as it is. The discipline of covenant morality, they might say, is a way of trying to avoid such a task and responsibility. For different reasons, both schools of thought are therefore ready to question and set aside some of the traditional moral limits of Christian ethics.

Enjoying the Goodness of Created Things

The goodness of God's gifts in the created world call for our respect and enjoyment. There is a right understanding, which values the gifts God has given, without setting our hearts on them and putting them in God's place as the object of affection and worship. In contrast to the Christian approach, modern technological attitudes lead to two mistakes. On the one hand, the instrumental approach to natural things fails to offer them the respect they deserve. Technological man seeks to improve all the time on the given structures of nature, treating it with scant respect. Sometimes this leads people to celebrate, not the good gifts of nature, but the success of human ingenuity and the wonders of technological creativity. This is easily allied to the age-old human propensity to seek security and comfort in the amassing of personal property and wealth. On the other hand, many react against the barrenness of human remaking of the world by worshipping the natural world and its beauty.

The Judaeo-Christian tradition celebrates the goodness of the world, though the New Testament sees great danger in possessions. The point is not that enjoyment of good things is wrong, but that it is wrong to set our hearts on possessing them, on amassing them and keeping them for security or other reasons. The question then is: how can we understand our proper relationship with material things? Some of the Bible's themes about creation will help answer this question.

The ordered nature of creation demands human respect. There are senses in which it is appropriate to work with the grain of nature, not across it. This is a substantial issue in an age of large scale technology. But it does not necessarily provide full guidance. It does not mean, for instance that trees are not to be cut down, to provide wood for housing, or for warmth, or for other practical reasons, such as clearing land for agriculture. But it may make cutting down trees on a large or a small scale a real question.

Both to see how human use of natural things is justified, and to see the limits on human dominion, we need to think about the purposes which God intends created things to serve. As we have seen, the good order of creation implies first of all that God's creatures are to be respected in their own right. Things have value simply for their own sake. But beyond this, they are also given to humanity to be used as well as cared for. Plants, vegetables and fruits are given for food (though the Bible at no point appears to require vegetarianism, it is very much more reserved than to say that animals are given for human food). Minerals in the ground are there to be mined, land to be cultivated, fish to be caught, wood to be cut and used, and so on. Use as well as improvement of the land is intended for human provision.

Things are to be used diligently and well, in order that we should provide for ourselves and for others.

A **technological approach** has a highly instrumental approach to material things. Things are there to provide for human beings to use or dispose of, to cherish or transform, just as they see fit. The doctrine of creation leads Christians to value things more highly than this. At the same time, Christians are warned by Jesus to have a carefree attitude to possessions. This is not a paradox, nor is it really a tension or balance between two opposites. It is merely a matter of the proper attitude to one who gives a gift. Gifts can play an important part in friendships and in families. The one who gives hopes that the gift will be warmly received, that it will please the receiver, and be valued by them. But the giver does not expect that the gift itself will command all the attention of the one who receives it. Even when we give to children, although we know that they are more interested in the gift for a while, we teach them to thank the giver, not to ignore them. Created things are God's gift to us. There is a persistent danger that we are so pleased with creation, with our mastery of it and enjoyment of it, that we turn from God himself. The asceticism which Jesus taught and practised is meant to underline this, not to devalue the goodness of life. Our enjoyment of nature's goodness is finally pointless if it is not set in the context of a real and grateful relationship with God the giver.

The purposes of created things are to be learned by recognising the creation themes we have examined — the goodness of creation, its ordering, our autonomy and responsibility within it, and so on. But things, and property, also have a context in human society, in our relationships with each other, as well as with God. To get a full and proper picture of the covenant ethic of property, we will need both the doctrines of creation and covenant love.

Six

Creation and Covenant

It is time to bring together the two major themes which underlie Christian ethics. In joining covenant love and creation we reach the heart of Christian ethics. With a firm grasp at this point we will be able to illuminate many of the main areas of ethics. Above all it is important to articulate the two foundations correctly, and this can only be done by relating them to each other. Without this basis firmly in place ethics is likely to fall into trouble sooner or later.

We have seen that love is at the centre of God's nature, and love is to be the virtue which characterises our response to God. Covenant love is enduring, faithful, patient and forgiving. Secondly, we have explored some implications of the belief that God created the world with definite intentions, and with pattern and purpose. Included in that pattern is a degree of autonomy for living creatures, and above all for human beings. Humanity has the task of consciously determining the way in which it will conform (or not) to the purposes God intends. Within God's created structures and purposes human beings have the opportunity to work out the meaning of their love.

At the heart of the Christian gospel is the message that God made people in order to love them, and that they might respond to his love. Love is the central plan behind God's creation. All Christians are familiar with this truth as a summary of God's plan of redemption, as the briefest possible description of the meaning of the life and death of Christ. This message is at the heart of Christian ethics as well as of the gospel. Much of Christian ethics can be understood as an outworking of the meaning of Christian love for one's neighbour. We have begun to ask about the created goodness of marriage, and of natural things. In this chapter we will bring these two themes together.

What does it mean for our understanding of love that it is embodied in this world, in the patterns of God's creation? How do these patterns point us towards fulfilment of God's purposes? In this chapter we will look briefly at how this works out in various topics, such as work, parenthood and so on. In the next chapter we will look at marriage.

Making the themes of creation and covenant the basis for ethics is an idea we owe to Karl Barth.[1] We can summarise his essential idea quite simply. As he put it, covenant love is the meaning, the fulfilment of creation. At the same time, creation is the basis, the presupposition for covenant. Barth used a simple image — a circle with a centre and a circumference — to explain his thought. Covenant is the centre, the hub. This is the point to which all the points on the circumference are directed, the centre from which the whole is understood. The circumference is the essential embodiment of the circle, without which it has no reality. Love is embodied and expressed in created physical reality. But creation's meaning has to be seen in covenant. It was in order to express his love that God created the world. Creation is a reality in which love can find embodiment.

Barth's expression can be worked out in different areas of life. We will find as we do so some of the benefits of this way of approaching the foundations for ethics. The centrality of covenant love shapes and controls the way in which we approach nature. So, for instance, an emphasis on creation can lead to a very passive acceptance of the status quo. We can so emphasise the goodness of what has come into being that we do not look sufficiently for its transformation. A positive emphasis on creation can also lead us to overlook the gospel concern for our relationship to God. The things of the world can obscure the need for discipleship, which sometimes demands self-denial. We may place too great an emphasis on marriage and family life, forgetting the fact that these are not God's only or best blessing. Or we may come to see earthly prosperity too simply as God's blessing, again forgetting the impermanence of worldly wealth. Emphasising the priority of covenant love will mean that the message of the gospel has its proper authority in ethics.

But without the doctrine of creation, the idea of love can lack shape and solidity. Love can mean many different things. In particular, one

---

[1] See particularly *Church Dogmatics* III, i.

danger is to spiritualise love so that it loses contact with the earthly realities of human life. Without a strong affirmation of created order, an emphasis on love can lead to a desire to transform and remake the world in new and radical ways, ways that can be too careless of flesh and blood realities. Love's concern to transform and redeem needs to recognise that there is an existing order to be changed, which makes demands as well as offering possibilities. Insisting that love must be expressed in created reality can save us from overlooking the vulnerable who so easily suffer when love gets carried away as feeling or impulse.

The two themes of creation and covenant, and the clear connection between them, provide virtually the complete basis for our understanding of ethics. It is from this point that we will gain insight into a wide range of questions. It is from this standpoint that we will understand how the various authorities for our moral decisions fit together — for example, moral laws, biblical commands, and conscience. But before we go on to these and other topics, we can sketch the way this approach makes sense of several areas we usually take for granted.

As we will see, the point is not that creation and covenant provide any new kind of morality. The language may be unfamiliar, but the basic intention is at the heart of long-standing Christian views. However, those views need to be grasped and explained in new ways to meet the radical new questions being asked. The best way to show this is to look at a number of familiar and relatively non-controversial topics. In this chapter we will consider truth-telling, work, parents and children, property and technology. The next chapter, more controversially, will look at some of the issues around sex and marriage.

Truth and the Gift of Speech

Understanding even our most apparently obvious moral rules requires that we find out why such rules are given. The example of the rule that we should always tell the truth provides a good example of this. Earlier, we looked at the best way of expressing and understanding the moral rule against lying. Now we will see how that expression makes sense within the perspective of creation and covenant.

At the root of the Christian emphasis on honesty and truth telling is the belief in the God who speaks, and whose word is absolutely true and trustworthy. This is so well known that we hardly need to dwell on it. In the beginning, God created by his word. 'God said 'Let there be light', and there was light'. The Gospel of John introduces Jesus Christ by speaking of him as the Word of God. 'From the very beginning the Word was with God. Through him God made all things'. . . . 'The Word became a human being and, full of grace and truth, lived among us'. What God says expresses his very being, in action, in communication, and in Jesus Christ. It is no wonder therefore that the Psalms (for instance) make so much of the faithfulness, the truthfulness, and the reliability of God's word, as well as its authority. For the Judaeo–Christian tradition, God's word is expressed in the sacred books of the Old and New Testaments. The Christian faith is thus marked at every point by its character as a faith which is expressed in word, in communication; a word which reliably informs about the nature of God and his will.

Human beings who are to be truly like God must therefore be truthful. As God's word is a wholly reliable and accurate expression of himself, so human speech should be truthful. But truth is not only an end in itself. Speech also enables God to communicate. Human speech is a created gift for the building of community, for establishment of good relationships. The Genesis story of the Tower of Babel explains that when God wished to divide the human race, in order to curb its too high ambitions, he confused people by inventing different languages. More positively, the letter to the Ephesians emphasises that we should speak the truth out of love, to help one another and to do good (Eph. 4:25–29).

Two central principles of our speaking are that we should tell the truth, and that we should build our community life, establishing trust and relationships. For the most part, of course, these two go hand in hand. Indeed, moralists have often noted how lying leads to distrust, bringing about suspicion or enmity. But there are also occasions when simply telling the truth is not a way to do good. These vary greatly in significance, from the everyday to matters of life and death. Everyday politeness often requires us to conceal our feelings with conventional responses which may be the opposite of our inner emotions. We thank our hosts for their hospitality, even if we did not enjoy the food or the company. Medical staff know that it is not usually appropriate to give a very sick patient the whole truth about their condition until they are ready to hear it. Neither of these occasions demands that we actually say something blatantly untruthful, but we are clearly telling less than the whole truth. But there are occasions, for instance in warfare, when deliberate deceit actually seems morally required by our duty to protect the lives of our own forces. As we have seen, we can summarise these exceptions in the formula 'Never withhold the truth from one to whom it is due'.

All these occasions reveal that speaking the truth is not always a way of building trust and relationship, not always a way of doing good. The proper use of the created gift of speech is that it should communicate truth. This is important in its own right, but at the same time the purpose of communication is to promote our covenant relationships. In analysing difficulties, it helps if we return to the fundamental purposes. The question is how we can order our lives and our speech so as to bring together the respect for truth with love of our neighbour.

Work

Working life seems to present us with a series of contradictions. There are many who overwork, to the detriment of family and community life, while at the same time there are many able people unable to work because they cannot find employment. For many people work is strenuous and demanding, but though workers look forward to holidays, unemployment is feared almost above all else. Of course unemployment leads to poverty, but that is not the only reason why it seems such an evil. Work is essential to our lives and well-being, and it brings many rewards. But it is a dangerous exaggeration to say that work is the point of our lives. We do not simply live in order to work. On the other hand, it seems too cynical to say that we only work in order to live. Work is not mere drudgery, to be finished as soon as possible so that we can get on with the real business of life.

Creation and covenant offer an excellent way of holding some of these tensions together. Our work is the way in which we affirm the goodness of creation. By working we say yes to God's creation, as we provide the things necessary for one another, so that we may enjoy God's blessings. But we do not forget that the central purpose of creation is that we may know God's love, and reflect that love in our care for one another. The essential point of our work, then, is that we serve our neighbours, in affirming the goodness of their lives. We need the necessities of life, such as food, shelter, clothing, medicine, and transport, both for their own sake, and for the sake of our life together. It is a mistake to lay too much weight on one reason at the expense of the other. If we think that better food, or a more convenient house, is the point of our efforts, then our ambition is too limited. We should certainly see those things as good. But as created forms of God's good provision, they must not obscure the greater goodnesses of love, of service, of knowing God. At the same time, we should not overlook or despise created goodness, thinking that we should only be interested in spiritual matters.

We do not have to choose between the false dichotomy of either living to work, or working to live. Rather we should give ourselves diligently to our work, aiming in that work to serve our neighbour. In so doing we affirm our own existence, and the existence of those we serve. But our existence, though good in itself, is not an end in itself. The point of our created existence is to be found in covenant.

This understanding makes sense of our experience of work, and gives an excellent standpoint from which to appraise modern conditions of work. Work, as we know, is good in many ways. We are made for work, and often find it fulfilling and satisfying. It gives an important daily routine, and can give good opportunities for working together with others. Unemployment is unwelcome to most people, even if they do not need the money. But if it becomes the centre of our lives, to the exclusion of other things, then it is out of proportion. We cannot fulfil our lives as created beings without reference to God's overall plan for creation. If our work becomes the centre, squeezing out the rationale of love and service, then it is bound to seem an inadequate fulfilment. Work has its repetitive side, its drudgery, reflecting the fact that creation awaits redemption. It may well be that one of the reasons why unemployment is seen as such a threat is the tendency to overrate the importance of work. For instance, think of the way in which we so often classify people by their occupation.

We often tend to think of work simply as employment. But work is much more than the things we do to earn money. Most obviously, parents who stay at home to care for young children and other family members may easily work harder, certainly for longer hours, than those who go out to work! Perhaps the reason we make this mistake is that housework is unpaid. To be employed means being paid. For many employees it also gives the status of being part of the workings of a modern industrial economy, with all its power and productivity. Modern industry certainly gives its rewards to those who work in it, but it also makes its own characteristic demands on them. It has certain demands for efficiency, for functioning according to its own rules. It demands flexibility and mobility, as people have to change jobs, learn new skills, change their practices, and so on. A creation–covenant perspective is ready to question some of this. Do the laws of profit and the market always enable us to serve each other more effectively? Do they help us to affirm God's created world, or do they tend to ignore its goodness? The answers to these questions are not obvious, and they do not imply that modern industry is all bad. But the important point is that the conditions of good work are not simply decided by what pays best, or what makes the most profit. The profit motive is intended to show us the most efficient ways to do things. But that is not the only question to ask. More fundamentally, our work should affirm the goodness of God's creation, and affirm and prolong our existence as created beings.[2]

Covenant and Property

In considering God's purposes for created things, we have seen that one of the main themes is that we should use the good things to provide for ourselves and for each other. How this should be done

---

[2] Barth's analysis of 'The Active Life' (Church Dogmatics III, iv, 55.3, pp. 470–564) is still strikingly relevant, though first published in 1951. His note of warning about the proper attitude to work, under the headings of the reflectivity and limitation of work (pp. 545–64), exactly hits the mark.

will determine our attitude to the environment, to technology and science, and to the way things are owned and shared between people. The nature of human property may at first sight seem rather obvious, but in fact a good deal hangs on the way **property** is understood. What are the rights that go with ownership of property of different kinds, and what are the obligations? We will now look at the kind of view of property to which a covenant ethic leads. It will help in understanding this to contrast a covenant approach with the typically modern view of property.

The modern view of property is a highly instrumental and individualist one. The basic idea is typified by the method of land allocation used in the development of frontier territories in North America. The way of life is famously portrayed in Laura Ingalls Wilder's *Little House on the Prairie* books. Whenever new land was opened up to settlers, all the settler had to do was register a claim for an area of land. There was no payment for the land, but there was a crucial condition. Within a set period of time the settler had to establish his claim to the land by building on it, and by beginning to cultivate it.[3] This system provides the basic model for our modern property right, with one crucial exception. The model is this: that land or other things have no economic value until human effort is invested in them, to bring them under human control and transform them into saleable commodities by one means or other. It is the person who puts in the effective work of transformation who is entitled to be regarded as the owner. He then has the rights of ownership over what he has transformed.

The view of property rights that should emerge from this would imply that the owner has a strong responsibility to make his property fruitful, to care for it and look after it well. But instead, modern property rights confer absolute rights on the owner, who may neglect or use his property as he chooses. Any restriction on these rights tends to be regarded as some kind of interference with them. In principle, neither the property itself nor the rest of society has any direct claim on the way the property is used. Claims only arise when other kinds of rights are infringed, for instance when harm is done to other people

---

[3] See the story as told by Laura Ingalls Wilder in *By the Shores of Silver Lake*.

or their property. Essentially property confers rights, but does not of itself imply any duties or responsibilities. Property is mine to keep or dispose of, to use well or carelessly, for my own benefit or for the benefit of others.

By contrast, a covenant ethic is much more cautious about property as a natural right. Property is more than a necessary evil, but less than a fundamental good. Property is necessary in order that we may truly serve our neighbour. In practice, as Aquinas observed, property is essential in order that things are properly cared for. Each person needs at least some basic possessions to call their own, both to provide for our own needs, and in order to help provide for others also. Our love for one another is not the joining of disembodied spirits, but has to be expressed in practical ways of one sort or another, not all involving things, to be sure (for there are words and deeds of other kinds too).

A rather different example from that of the pioneer settler is appropriate. The example of the 'innkeeper's law' was noted by Paul Ramsey.[4] The duties of the innkeeper are clearly prescribed. Keeping an inn brings with it certain responsibilities as well as rights. An innkeeper is obliged to provide accommodation to travellers in need of it, provided that they have the means to pay. It is not open to the inn to turn people away, if it is inconvenient for some reason. The purpose of the inn existing at that particular place is to be available for guests, and this purpose is often prescribed in law. Now the principle of the innkeeper's law can easily be extended to all sorts of other property whose essential purpose is a public, not a private one.

The innkeeper's law, which is a fitting expression of a covenant ethic, puts a different appearance on property rights from the ethic suggested by the pioneer's claim. It makes explicit what is often tacitly acknowledged to be the case, namely that any substantial ownership of property brings with it duties and responsibilities. Ramsey put it like this:

> Here was none of that erroneous notion that a man without his fellow man, and with no duties towards him, can be the bearer of absolute rights and use property in any way he pleases. The 'innkeeper's law' said in effect that all must be served by any man who sets up an inn at the crossroads that weary travellers reach by nightfall, since, having established there as owner, he now occupies

---

[4] In *Christian Ethics and the Sit-In.*

the space that otherwise might be held by an owner whose practice would be more in accord with natural justice or with the requirements of man's life with man. Man's destiny as a creature made in the image of God — in the image of God's fellow humanity — affects any of those inalienable rights he may be said to possess. . . . The 'innkeeper's law' manifests the fact that the political order with its justice and its law and a man's proper relation to the things he owns are the external basis, the promise, the possibility and capability for covenant-community.[5]

It is not possible to pursue here the implications of this different approach for our economic life. We can note that the two approaches are not totally contrasted. Both recognise private property rights; the innkeeper, after all, is entitled to be fully paid for his service. I think it is also true that capitalist economics recognises that public property brings duties with it. Even if these duties are imposed by regulation, instead of by economic incentive, they are still quite clearly imposed. (Neither the owner of the brewery, nor of the inn, is allowed to sell watered down beer or whisky!) When such duties are merely encouraged by economic incentive, we must remember too that capitalist economics sees it as a duty to pursue profits. In fact, observing some capitalists at work, making money seems to have something of the sacred about it! But both covenant and modern property rights do actually recognise a balance that has to be struck.

Enshrining a covenant property ethic in economic theory or economic legislation would be a matter requiring technical expertise. But it is clear that a different attitude is required by the acknowledgement that property ownership includes certain duties. Whatever the balance of capitalist freedom and social provision at a particular time and place, it always remains open to the property owner to use his or her property as if it was held in trust for others, rather than simply as a private affair.

Technology and the Environment

One of the reasons for the renewed interest in the doctrine of creation today is the need to formulate an accurate response to the questions posed by modern technology. What kind of ecological understanding

---

[5] *Ibid.*, p. 18.

is warranted by Christian faith? Should we, for instance, adopt a hands-off policy, thinking that we should not attempt to transform the goodness of God's creation into something better? Or should we, at the other extreme, leave no stone unturned in the quest to bring creation under human dominion? A different question is posed by the medical technologies which give much greater control over the beginnings and endings of human life. How should we respond to the experimental and theoretical research which is actively pursued in genetics and human aging? It seems at first sight that the biblical writings, which could know nothing of such questions, cannot possibly help us here. But the themes we have outlined do give us foundations for thought.

There is, of course, a huge difference in scale between the mining technology of Old Testament times and the modern technology of the nuclear age, of the electronic age. There is a decisive difference, for instance, in the harnessing of natural energy and putting it to work in powerful and sophisticated machines. Most would agree that there is a qualitative difference between modern coal mining and that of Job's time; there is also a bigger difference in the use to which that coal is put. There is an even greater difference between the social organisation of ancient industry and modern industry. Today's industry achieves quite new possibilities by virtue of modern economics, modern administration and communications. But the question we still have to ask is whether modern society is any wiser than ancient society. Clearly it is more ingenious, but the ancient writers spoke clearly of the difference between ingenuity and wisdom.

Many contemporary strands of thought also call attention to this difference as we experience it today. There is an obvious gulf between the ingenuity of modern weaponry, and the plans and decisions of those who use it. Conflict among nations is as endemic as ever, but a great deal more violent and destructive. Advances in economic organisation and productivity have brought many benefits. But is it wise to commit our human destiny to the runaway juggernaut of economic progress? Worldwide, poverty and malnutrition are as widespread as ever. Debt and unemployment hang over many people in almost every country, cutting them off in cruel ways from the progress enjoyed by others. Our inability to understand, let alone control, the effects of modern economic life on the global ecology, speaks not merely of limits to our ingenuity but also questions the extent of our wisdom.

It is perhaps too easy a comment to compare the superb technological ability displayed in modern computing or television technology with the utterly banal uses to which they are so often put. It is hard to think that the pinnacle of humanity is represented by watching a contemporary TV quiz show, or playing a video game. Indeed, the contrast between the ingenuity required to invent a video game and the triviality of playing it makes the contrast between cleverness and wisdom as clear as it could be.

Critics like Jacques Ellul[6] and Ivan Illich[7] have pursued their critiques of modernity in much greater depth than is possible here. While ruthlessly critical, and often pessimistic, they recognise that it is by no means possible to return to some mythical golden age. The best we can do is try to identify as accurately and profoundly as we can the nature of the modern world. Anthony Giddens likens the progress of modernity to a juggernaut, a huge machine which men tried to ride and control, but which careers along in an unpredictable fashion, no matter what lies in its path.[8] Ellul emphasises in a dramatic and sometimes one-sided way that technology has its own momentum. It is illusory, he argues, to think that this momentum is under control, for in fact it is the technological method which now shapes the world.

What would biblical wisdom have to teach us in the face of this diagnosis? It is certainly a diagnosis with which many biblical writers would quickly feel at home. Isaiah's critique of idolatry lampoons those who cut down a tree, burn half of it as fuel, and carve the other half into an idol for worship. There is a somewhat similar dynamic in Isaiah's picture of idolatry and in the power of modern technology. In both it is the work of human hands to which humanity entrusts her own destiny. But if our modern prophets are right, it is even harder to escape from our modern gods than it was to escape idolatry in ancient Israel. The ancient writers' advice might be this: in order to

---

[6] *The Technological Society*, tr. J. Wilkinson.
[7] In books such as *Deschooling Society, Limits to Medicine, Gender*.
[8] In *The Consequences of Modernity*, pp. 139ff.

escape the power of idols, they must first be recognised for what they are. They have no ultimate benefits to offer, for ultimately they are powerless. They cannot confer love or wisdom, true insight or knowledge of true human destiny. In this light it is possible to speak truthfully, not trying to dismiss the results of human labour and ingenuity. Nor on the other hand will we dismiss the very real dangers. In the light of a sober estimate of modern society, we will be better able to worship God single-mindedly, and love and serve one another. We will be able to see that it is neither the triumphs nor the disasters of modern life that ultimately matter so much as the patient honest living of the people of God on pilgrimage.

Parents and Children

Until recently it would have been possible to say that the basic shape and purpose of **parenthood** was too obvious to need discussing. A man and a woman join together in marriage, and from their union may come children. Those children remain in their care and nurture until adulthood. Some followed Thomas Aquinas in seeing in the needs of children a good argument for permanent monogamous marriage. Only in such a marriage could the necessary stability be found within which children would find their needs for security and other things met.

At the end of the twentieth century much less of this can be taken for granted. Three key developments can be mentioned. First, **marriage** is widely challenged as the only appropriate context for bringing up children. Although there would seem little doubt that a stable and secure home life is more conducive to children's well-being than an unstable and insecure one, this does not settle the question. It is asked whether a single parent cannot provide a good home, assuming that singleness does not entail poverty or social deprivation. Alternatively, why should a committed gay or lesbian couple not provide just as good an upbringing as a heterosexual couple? Second, new **reproductive technologies** have altered for ever the basic truth that a child has only two biological parents, and widened the possibilities for the biological parents not being the nurturing parents. Third, various trends have served to emphasise the **rights and independence of children**. It cannot be assumed, as it largely was a generation ago, that children ought to respect adults, and obey those who are responsible for them, including parents, teachers and others. Instead, children are seen as bearing rights of self-determination, with the result that the transition from childhood to adulthood is very difficult to identify. Rather than it being seen as a good thing for children to be taught religious faith, the assumption that they should make their own choices gains ground. Even in the earliest school years, some see it as an imposition to assume that their faith will be the faith of their family or community.

Clearly we have to think more deeply about the meaning of parenthood. In this area, as in others, we have to exercise a good deal of caution. We have to be careful that we do not simply identify prevalent social customs as the invariable purpose of God. Similarly we also have to be careful not to set too narrow a limit on our responsibility to interpret and transform the created conditions of life. If, for instance, we can find genuinely better methods of human reproduction, we would need good reasons not to use them. But this proper caution must not prevent us from thinking through the purposes of God for the continuance of the human race.

We can begin from the obvious but now outdated certainty that sexual intercourse could not be separated from procreation. Men and women, like other living creatures, were created by God to multiply. Until recently, procreation was not possible without sex, and sex was generally inseparable from the prospect of procreation. But it is by no means obvious that we should deduce a firm moral rule from this, quite apart from the issue of **contraception**. Sex does not always lead to procreation; there have always been those unable to conceive and bear children. Nor is procreation in itself a necessary qualification for bringing up children. Many single people, without natural children, have cared for children born to others, whether as orphans or for other reasons.

However, we should pause before we dismiss the link between sex and procreation. We must ask if the link is a mere biological accident which can now be overcome. The themes of creation and covenant indicate that there is more to the link than simply biology. The connection between sexual love and procreation can be seen as highly significant. The way in which parents procreate out of their love for one another can be seen as a reflection of the way God's love is the source of his creation. That children are brought into being within a context of love is not merely an accident of biology. Rather, the created biology of family life points very surely to the centrality of love.

Our main reason for caution must be that it would be unwise to make absolute rules in this area.[9] (One can compare this caution with principles about respect for truth, or respect for human life, for instance. In those matters it is possible to specify exceptions to binding rules with a good deal of precision.) In respect of parents and children, one can only look for a broad understanding. The understanding we should have is that God's gift to many wives and husbands is for them to bear children. They do not do this as a matter of course, but in order to extend the possibilities for God's love and for human love. Children are given to us as a sign of hope, and as a promise that God continues to love humankind. Normally then, parents have the responsibility to bring up their children in faith, hope and love.

How do we approach the modern questions? The purpose of the link between sex and procreation is easily read in the light of creation and covenant. The created gift of child-bearing is set within the love of parents, one for another and for their children. But this cannot rule out the very real possibility that other loving and secure contexts may also provide a good place to bring up children. Such possibilities should be considered on their merits, both from the moral point of view, and from the social and legal point of view. Nor can we rule out the possibility that there may be other perfectly acceptable ways of conceiving children, other than through sexual intercourse. Again, the key moral question (from this point of view) is whether children so conceived will be brought up in a good context.[10]

The normal context for the upbringing of children is the family unit, centred on the married couple, mother and father. But this is not a universal rule. The themes of creation and covenant also have

---

[9] Cf. our comment above Chapter 4, e.g. pp. 51, 57–9.

[10] Of course there are other moral questions about new reproductive technologies, which we do not consider here.

something to say about the status of children. The creation theme reminds us that children are indeed children, not little adults. They need and deserve a form of love, respect and treatment which is appropriate to them. This may sound obvious, but our culture is prone to overlook the creaturely realities. In the case of children, the modern risk is to think of them as little autonomous individuals, rather than as those who are growing up into maturity and adulthood. It is therefore right to expect children to defer to parents (and others), in ways appropriate to their age. As Stanley Hauerwas has pointed out, this means Christian parents not being afraid to expect their children to adopt their Christian faith.[11] Children are not autonomous, to make decisions of faith, and other matters, from the outset. In the transition from childhood to adulthood, clearly there is a handover of such matters from parents to children – defining the handover is a classically perennial debate!

The themes of creation and covenant provide the basis on which we can think and rethink the shape of our lives. We have looked at a number of such areas — truth, work, property, ecology and parenthood. But the most obvious example is marriage, which we will consider next.

---

[11] For instance in *A Community of Character*, ch. 9.

Seven

Creation and Sexuality

There is a lively debate, both in society and in the church, about the place of marriage in our **sexual** lives. In fact, there are several linked debates, rather than just one. Recently there has been renewed questioning in the church about the propriety of sex before marriage, in the light of the general shift in social customs. The question of **divorce** and **remarriage**, by contrast, has been a matter of debate in the church for much longer, although this debate has also reflected social trends. Additionally, the moral legitimacy of **homosexual** relationships has been under discussion in the churches, and is currently a pressing topic again.[1] Here society is more sharply divided about the extent to which homosexuality should be considered socially acceptable.

A number of Christian theologians have recently challenged what they take to be the traditional Christian viewpoint. Scholarly and popular writers, tackling ethics generally, and specifically sex and marriage, have all pointed in similar directions. These are respected churchmen and theologians, including Keeling, Harvey, Brett and Thatcher.[2] Although in many respects there are real differences between them, it is possible to see a common thread, which runs back at least to the 1960s. **Responsibility** is one of the central themes in the critique of the tradition. We will call these critics of the tradition 'responsibilists'.[3]

---

[1] See for instance *Issues in Human Sexuality*, House of Bishops of the Church of England, or Michael Vasey, *Strangers and Friends*.

[2] Michael Keeling, *The Foundations of Christian Ethics;* Anthony Harvey, *Promise or Pretence?*; Paul Brett, *Love Your Neighbour;* Adrian Thatcher, *Liberating Sex.*

[3] This is my word: I have not been able to think of a better one to contrast with 'traditionalist'.

In order to survey the debate between responsibilists and traditionalists, we will first outline various criticisms of the traditional understanding of marriage. For the tradition to respond effectively to these criticisms, it is necessary to think more thoroughly about the meaning of sex and marriage. Our creation–covenant approach will provide a more convincing account than it is possible to give simply by repeating the traditional rules, whether in a legalistic or homiletic kind of way.

Responsibility as the Key Test

Those who emphasise the importance of human responsibility all tend to make the same essential points. First, sex is to be welcomed as a good gift. It is not to be feared or shunned, or regarded as essentially negative, mainly as a source of temptation. In our sexual activity, the main point is that we should behave responsibly. Sex is basically an expression of human love and affection in intimate physical relationship. We should seek to use our sexual gifts in creative and loving ways, seeking to build others up, not exploit them. Sex is a part of our human relationships, and it is possible to err by denying our sexuality as well as by using it carelessly. In forging a new ethic of **sexuality**, we should be ready to take advantage of the fact that sex and procreation are not inextricably linked, as they used to be. A new sexual ethic is typically more concerned to provide insight and guidelines, in order that people may freely make their own decisions. Rigid rules, they say, deny people's individual responsibility rather than encouraging them to exercise it fully.

This is not to deny that sex also has destructive possibilities. Responsibilists acknowledge these, and seek to place appropriate moral limits to head off the dangers. The essential criterion is that sex should be mutually upbuilding. This means that any sex in which one partner exploits or harms the other is to be considered morally illegitimate. For instance, this means that sex should always be with the full and understanding consent of both partners. This means that sex is for adults, as children are not in a place to give such consent. It means also that adultery is normally ruled out, as married couples have promised themselves exclusively to the other, and adultery breaks that relationship of trust. However, if the couple agree that either or both should enter into sexual relations with others (an 'open' marriage), then this is acceptable if harm is not done to either.

We can readily see how a responsibilist view works out in three key debates. On a typical responsibilist view, sex before marriage is not ruled out. Although promiscuous sex is very often exploitative and harmful, there is premarital sex which is not promiscuous. Certainly many people who live together before formally getting married can hardly be said to be exploiting each other. At the very least, for the church to continue to stand against the practice of anticipating the formal wedding ceremony is merely to insist on a negative and outdated legalism. There are many reasons why social customs have changed, and they do not simply have to do with moral indiscipline, let alone promiscuity. For instance, couples getting married increasingly pay for the wedding themselves.

As for divorce, responsibilists argue that there can be no definite rule against this. Some divorces are no doubt harmful to one partner. For instance the husband who abandons his wife for a more attractive young woman, probably the kind of situation Jesus had in mind in his condemnation of divorce, is still to be condemned. But it is unlikely that Jesus had in mind the situation which can arise when a marriage relationship turns sour, and is of no benefit to either partner. Here, a divorce which sets two people free from a trap which is preventing both from positive growth and hinders mature human life, is to be welcomed rather than condemned. When both husband and wife wish to be released from the promises they made to each other, in different times, perhaps many years previously, why should others insist that they hold together? In this light, the promise of permanence almost seems more like a trap than a joyful commitment. If there is regret, as there usually is, this is for the circumstances which led to divorce, not for the divorce which sets two people free.

As for homosexuality, responsibilists again argue that the main criterion is that of avoiding exploitation or harm. Most would argue that more committed relationships are much to be preferred to casual or short lived affairs. But there seems no good reason, on this account of morality, to draw any substantial distinction in principle between homosexual and heterosexual love. It is possible to acknowledge that the Bible does not approve of homosexuality, while still arguing that the grounds for seeing the Bible as establishing heavy prohibitions are often exaggerated. The Bible was, it is argued, unaware of the way in which a homosexual orientation is deeply built into some people's make-up, with its roots, so far as we can tell, in individual genetic make-up as well as the indelible effects of significant events in the earliest years of life. The Bible's condemnations, such as they are, are to be read as attacks on a way of life which dishonours our lives by a casual or idolatrous approach to sexual expression.

This line of thought represents a substantial challenge to a traditional covenant understanding of sexuality. In response, the tradition is forced to a re-examination of the theological themes of covenant love and creation. It is important to begin by emphasising that Christian ethics looks first to Jesus. In looking at the ethics of marriage it seems natural to begin with Genesis. While convenient, the danger of starting with the creation story is that we relegate Jesus' praise of celibacy to a footnote. For Jesus, service of the kingdom was a higher priority than marriage. In defending marriage against critics, Christians have to be careful to remember that marriage is an earthly affair. In heaven 'there is neither marriage nor giving in marriage'. We need to praise marriage, but not to overpraise it, and certainly not in comparison to the single state.

The traditional account cannot be saved simply by repeating the biblical commands and prohibitions as they are. The reason for this is implicit in the approach taken by the responsibilist argument. The argument is that biblical commands were appropriate ways in that time and culture of expressing the values of promoting maturity, and preventing harm and exploitation. Nor is it enough for traditionalists to point to the dangers of greater sexual freedom. These are admitted by responsibilists, but their point is that to refuse the responsibilities of greater freedom is also to refuse our calling to maturity and growth. We should not any longer seek to prevent people from making their own decisions, no longer seek to keep them in a kind of moral childhood.

Creation, Covenant and Marriage

Bearing in mind all the time that creation is approached from the
teaching of Jesus, we turn back to the Genesis account of creation:
'So God created human beings, making them to be like himself. He
created them male and female' (Gen. 1:27–8). Some commentators
have suggested, looking at the parallelism which places 'The image of
God' side by side with 'Male and female', that it is our complementary
sexuality which makes us like God.[4] The implication is that the
difference creates special possibilities for relationship, which reflect
God's loving nature. A complementary account of the creation of man
and woman, with a very different feel, is given in the second chapter.
This is the story of God making woman from the body of the man.
The story emphasises the special closeness of man and woman 'Bone
taken from my bone, flesh taken from my flesh' (ch 2:23). The writer
adds 'That is why a man leaves his father and mother and is united
with his wife, and they become one' (2:24). Here the writer offers an
explanation for marriage in his story of God's creation.

These stories assume special significance for Christian understanding because of the use to which they are put at crucial points in
the New Testament. Jesus referred to both the passages in his answers
to questions about divorce. In his letters to the Corinthians (1 Cor.11),
St Paul relies on both passages for his understanding of the roles of
men and women, and their relationships in the church. Our defence
of the tradition must begin here.

Marriage offers the most obvious illustration of covenant and
creation. In the creation of men and women God created the
possibility for human relationships of a special kind. The relationship
of marriage is deliberately compared in the Bible to the relationship
of God and his people. Marriage offers a way in which our human
love can reflect God's love and fulfil his creative purposes. To explore
this further, we can examine the idea of **faithfulness**, which is central
to the Christian ethic of marriage, and the element perhaps most
questioned in contemporary society.

Faithfulness means at least two crucial things. It means permanence,
that a couple promise to stay together 'For better or worse', to the

---

[4]   Particularly following Karl Barth. See for instance *Church Dogmatics*, III, i, pp. 183–7.

end of their lives. It also means exclusivity, in that they reserve their intimate and complete trust for each other. Exclusivity, or monogamy, is usually taken to apply to sexual intercourse being reserved for the marriage partner, but it can no doubt apply to other forms of close intimacy. As we have seen, the virtues of permanence and exclusivity in sexual life are questioned by many. Do these virtues still belong to marriage in the present age?

Lifelong faithfulness is in question partly because people live longer today than they used to. Most marriages now have to survive for many more years than they might have expected in earlier generations. Increased life expectancy has combined with a variety of other pressures, including greater social mobility, increased material freedom, and higher ideals for married love. The effect of these changes has been to leave many people in marriages which are increasingly experienced as frustrating rather than fulfilling. With divorce a practical possibility, it is natural to ask what is to be gained from remaining in a situation from which nobody seems to gain. The only thing holding the marriage together is the mutual commitment which began it. If both wish to be released from that promise, then why should they remain permanently locked together in frustration?

The protest against faithfulness is more common than the protest against exclusiveness. Most people do not wish to live in polygamous arrangements, at least from the point of view of sharing a partner with other husbands or wives. Nevertheless, there are some who are happy, whether openly or tacitly, for their spouse to engage in sexual relationships with others. If everyone is happy, the question is why open marriage should be morally condemned.

The themes of covenant and creation supply a twin answer to these objections to the traditional view of marriage. From a creation point of view, we can say that a permanent and exclusive relationship in marriage is one of the fulfilments of God's purposes in making people as men and women. As such, the claim is that this pattern of living is one that will prove most suitable and fulfilling, for individuals and for society. In our own day, it is striking to note how high ideals for marriage lead lovers to promise undying fidelity. Indeed the quest for intimacy in modern society goes beyond the covenant ideal in some ways, in the way that it puts so much weight on the relationship between married partners. We should note that this quest for intimacy is derived in part from the Christian ideal. The idea, then, that men and women are made by God with marriage in mind seems to fit with widespread human experience. But the doctrine of creation does not supply the whole story.

Covenant love finds an obvious expression in marriage. The love between husband and wife is compared in scripture to God's love for his people. 'Husbands, love your wives just as Christ loved the church and gave his life for it' (Eph. 5:25). It is this which is at the root of the high Christian ideal. The promise of permanence, and sticking by that promise, enables couples to rely on one another for support in times of weakness and vulnerability. Sickness and misfortune comesto many of us, and death comes to us all. In fulfilling the ideal of faithfulness, we are able to stick by one another. Paul Ramsey wrote eloquently on this theme:

> It was married faithfulness, cut to the measure of God's own faithfulness, that opened the possibility of permanent, lifelong partnership as the meaning of the marriage covenant. It was the inseverability of Christ's covenant with us that, touching the covenants among men, made for the inseverability of the marriage bond.
>
> Just as we know the heart and needs of a stranger from God's care for us while we were yet strangers, we also know the heart and need of a dying one from God's care for us who live always in the midst of death. This means that the perfection of love is the working knowledge of another as a creature of flesh and blood whose fate is to live always in the valley of the shadow of death. . . This is why the marriage vow proposes provisionally to take hold of the shadow of death upon the human countenance and promises permanence 'Till death us do part'. If this is not so, there is found in marriage no 'helper' fit to the human condition; and, Christians believe, there is no marriage that has been touched by God's perduring love.[5]

Ramsey regarded this as close to the heart of Christian ethics. Furthermore, those very promises hold us to one another and restrain us. Maybe they can hold us when we are tempted away, and maybe they can help to prevent temptation from arising, as we insist on regarding those promises as sacrosanct. There is no doubt that in a society with a high divorce rate, it becomes harder for married couples

---

[5] 'The Biblical Norm of Righteousness', pp. 428–9.

to preserve their own marriages, since the solidity of the marriage commitment comes under greater question generally.

The covenant basis of marriage is found in the love of Christ for his people. It is vital that we learn our view of marriage from this vantage point, for the Old Testament outlook can imply that the single or childless are seriously deprived of an essential aspect of life. Jesus himself both taught and demonstrated that love for others does not imply the necessity of marriage or children. In fact, his example has led the church from time to time to regard marriage as a way of life somehow second-class by comparison with celibacy.[6] Perhaps inevitably, the desire to imitate the celibate life lived by Jesus, a way of life that led to the fullest demonstration of God's love, meant that celibacy would be seen as more commendable than marriage. However, the choice of marriage or singleness should be seen as matter of vocation, not a question of moral preference. There seems no need to regard singleness or marriage as morally better or worse than one another. Either way, it is clear that both are regarded in the light of covenant love as highly demanding ways of life.

Christian tradition has filled out the ideal of the goodness of permanent monogamous marriage by pointing to an additional advantage. This is not the primary reason for the marriage ideal, but belongs very aptly with creation and covenant principles. Marital faithfulness provides a good basis for bringing up children. It offers security, serves as a good model for relationships and personal commitment, and for education in social roles. The overall experience of single-parent families, that it is generally much harder to bring up children well on one's own, bears this out. Thomas Aquinas made this argument a key reason for marriage.

Before we see how the covenant–creation perspective enables us to defend the main lines of the traditional view, we need to summarise what it implies for the central meaning of a marriage. At the heart of a marriage is the covenant union of the husband and wife. The centre of marriage is that both freely consent to enter that union. This union is better called a covenant, than a contract. The difference between a covenant and a contract is that the covenant is modelled on the covenant love of God. This means, for instance, that in some key

---

[6] In contrast to the view prevalent today that it is singleness which is second-class.

respects the nature of the union is given, rather than being agreed between the partners. It is a given that the union should be permanent and exclusive.

The detailed ways in which the marriage relationship is expressed obviously vary considerably. For instance, the ways in which they share money, the roles they take up in work and in domestic life and so on, which are often strongly prescribed by social custom, are not invariable. There are three elements normally common to marriage. First, the couple live and share together. Second, they are united in sexual intimacy and intercourse. Thirdly, their union is publicly and legally recognised, and this recognition normally takes place at a wedding ceremony. These three elements are the normal way in which the marriage relationship is expressed, for any married couple. The absence of any one is liable to weaken the marriage. But it is important to notice that none of these three things actually makes a marriage, on its own. Nor does their absence necessarily mean that there is no marriage.

The covenant and creation view of marriage offers a high ideal for marriage. It is an ideal shaped above all by the concern to see the love of God reflected in human relationships. But it is an ideal embodied in a social pattern which does justice to the way in which human beings are made. The desire for reliable, faithful, loving relationships seems to be expressed by people in all sorts of cultures. Although marriage patterns vary quite widely in different societies, it is remarkable how great are the similarities from one place to another. Christians can offer the covenant ideal, knowing that it is a true interpretation of some of the deepest wishes of created human beings.

The Tradition's Response

We can now see how the traditional doctrine arrives at its answers to the three questions of sex before marriage, divorce, and homosexuality. The question of 'sex before marriage' concerns the transition from singleness to marriage. The decision to marry is of crucial importance, as it has such unique and lifelong implications. Societies have their own customs and provisions for this transition. Customs and ceremo-

nies have an important public and social role. They are also designed
to help young people make wise decisions, understanding the meaning
of what they are committing themselves to. The point of the traditional prohibition of sex before marriage is that it brings together the
formal act of commitment, the start of living together, and the
complete sexual intimacy of intercourse, at the same event. All these
are expressions of the mutual commitment which the couple make to
one another. Although social customs are changing, there is still merit
in the older traditions. When sexual intercourse and living together
happen as the first stages of the commitment, followed some time later
by the public ceremony, there is much more room for ambiguity about
the nature of the commitment. It is quite clear that many people live
and sleep together without any intention of marriage, while others
either intend a marriage commitment, or grow into it. Some people
argue that it is good to learn by going through a series of relationships
before entering marriage. However, since the promise of permanence
and faithfulness are at the heart of marriage, it is not really possible to
experiment or practice for this commitment. The evidence is that
those who experiment with premarital sex are more rather than less
likely to divorce.[7]

Divorce is a denial of the ideal of permanence in the marriage
commitment. Clearly, then, divorce represents some kind of failure.
Traditionalists differ on the way the church should uphold the ideal;
there are sharply contrasting views on the conditions, if any, under
which the church should ever countenance divorce and remarriage.
We shall return to this question in the chapter on forgiveness.

Homosexual Marriage?

The traditional view sees the marriage commitment as the appropriate
place for the full intimacy of sexual intercourse. Since this is one of
the questions asked about the ethics of homosexuality, we should
indicate the rationale of the traditional approach. One way of express-

---

[7] See for instance Tim Stafford, *Sexual Chaos*, p. 116. However, it needs to be noted that
statistics do not prove cause and effect. Cohabiting in itself is probably not the cause of
instability in the marriage. It is more likely that those who cohabit have the kinds of attitude
to marriage which later make separation and divorce more likely.

ing this is to ask whether there is a homosexual analogy to marriage. Some claim that this is possible — a lifelong commitment of two people of the same sex to live and share together in all aspects of life, which can be compared to the commitment of husband and wife. There is certainly no reason at all to deny that such a friendship is a happy and fulfilling way of life for some, perhaps many, homosexual couples. But I do not think that the structure of Christian thought allows this to be seen as analogous to marriage. The Bible indicates that it is part of the Creator's intention that a marriage is between a man and a woman, and that a friendship between two people of the same sex cannot be compared to marriage. If the tradition should be reinterpreted on the question of homosexuality, then homosexual marriage is not the best way forward.[8]

God's purpose in creating men and women is to make possible the committed and intimate relationship we call marriage. Only within this context can the goodness of sex find its true place. Sex is good, but like every other good thing it needs to find its right place in the larger scheme of things. When sex is commended without regard for the wider context of human life, it is in real ways dehumanised, and can work to dehumanise people and make them something less than they could be. So, it is in the marriage relationship that children are conceived, and the marriage provides the basis for family life within which children can be brought up.

It is clear that we have only surveyed rather sketchily the contrast between two approaches to sexual ethics. We have labelled these the traditional and the responsibilist. Our aim has not been to give a full account of their arguments. All we have seen, centrally, is a contrast between the view which sees certain patterns of behaviour as belonging within the structure of creation, and the view which emphasises the human responsibility to shape our lives so as to grow as fully as possible, while not harming or exploiting others.

---

[8] I am only too well aware that these brief comments are inadequately defended, especially with reference to the lively debate in the churches at the time of writing. See Michael Vasey, *Strangers and Friends*, which makes the point that the tradition is by no means as univocal as is usually assumed. He also points out that the contemporary culture of masculinity, and of friendship, leaves a lot to be desired.

Christian Marriage in a Secular Society

If the marriage ideal owes so much to convinced Christian belief, should we be more reluctant to urge such a religious ideal on a secular society? We must at least acknowledge the question. There is a tendency still to think of marriage patterns simply as a cultural heritage, not recognising the amount they owe to Christian beliefs and assumptions. Some would argue that Christians should, as it were, keep their beliefs and ethics to themselves. Since that would apply to marriage as much as to medicine, Sunday trading or pornography, might it be suggested that Christians should no longer argue for covenant marriage as part of our law?

To some extent this is presently a lost cause. Biblical ideals of purity of life are certainly not accepted in secular society, though they are not entirely obliterated either. So many divorces have an air of inevitability about them that it seems unforgiving and unhelpful to insist that it is never right to remarry after divorce. (We will consider later whether divorce can ever be seen as the right course, from an explicitly Christian point of view. For now we just note that the road leading to so many divorces, while perhaps individually inevitable in some sense, could hardly be applauded on Christian moral grounds.) While Christian teaching and witness will oppose these trends as vigorously as possible, it is hard to see how legislation can reintroduce practices based on Christian ideals. But this is not the whole story. After all, a substantial, if declining, minority of couples still freely choose to marry in churches (even if their motives are a mixture of belief, custom and sentiment). More seriously, the faithful marriage still provides the best framework for bringing up children in an individualist culture. The commitment to faithfulness still apparently serves a majority of married couples well. In the absence of any other basis on which shared social patterns of partnership and family life can be built, there seems every reason to try to maintain Christian ideals, at least in some form. The alternative ideal, that individuals should simply live by their own choices, making and breaking commitments as a matter of personal choice, seems much less attractive. It offers little prospect of social cohesion, an unhappy, shifting, environment for children to grow up in, and little protection for the more vulnerable with fewer inner resources.

Eight

Covenant, Creation and Moral Rules

We have now laid the foundations for a theory of Christian morality. The central point is that morality is to be understood in the light of belief in God as creator and lover of the world. The morality that follows from this belief is not arbitrary command, on the one hand, nor is it human invention, on the other. Rather it is to be discerned and understood by human beings, as they respond to their knowledge of God, in his love and creation. So far, we have outlined what it means to say that our love is to be like God's love, what it means to see the world as God's creation, and how we are to understand these two themes together, each in the light of the other. We have also begun to see how this perspective works out in some areas of morality, especially truth-telling and marriage.

In considering truth-telling, we saw that it is possible to understand a firm rule about truth, in a way that does justice to the many complexities of real human lives. In this chapter we can take a step further in seeing what part rules play in Christian ethics. In doing so we will complete the main structure of our understanding. We bring together a number of elements which cannot really be separated. First, the belief in creation gives us knowledge of regularities and consistencies, which give a basis for moral rules. The belief in covenant reinforces this basis, giving even more convincing reasons for coherence in our words and actions at different times and places. Second, the kind of moral rules we are looking for are determined by this creation–covenant foundation. Creation and covenant remain the fundamental point of reference in understanding and handling the specific principles, and laws. Third, we must clarify how moral rules are to be understood. We will do this in two ways, both of which point in the same direction. On the one hand, rules must accurately describe the human actions with which they are concerned. On the other hand, the meaning of moral rules can and must be clarified by referring back where necessary to their purposes – namely fulfilling the purposes of love and creation. Fourth, we can indicate how the use of moral rules in this setting avoids the dangers of moralism and legalism. The essential problem to be avoided here is that of taking moral rules out of context, not seeing them as part of a larger whole. Fifth, rules and the perfection to which they point must be understood in the light of human life as a whole. The ideal of human perfection is to be realised in frail and fallible human life. Moral thought is not to be confined to emphasis on individual rules, for its overall concern is that we should be shaped more and more as God had intended we should be.

Bringing these themes together in this chapter may appear somewhat theoretical and cryptic. There are some good reasons why a theoretical understanding is important. Our aim is to understand ethics, the reasons behind our moral thought and judgement. In doing this, we cannot afford to oversimplify. In many sorts of understanding some simplification is possible. But in dealing with morality everyone already works with a considerable degree of sophistication. For instance, it has already been noted that we have no trouble in telling fiction from lying. Fiction can convey truth very well, though it is all 'made up'.

Another reason why this chapter is of particular importance is that a number of attacks have been made on the usefulness and validity of moral rules. Rather than try to identify all the objections, and then trying to answer them all in detail, it seems more worthwhile to attempt to outline a positive view. The hope is that this may prove sufficiently substantial and convincing for the typical objections to fall to one side.

Of course, the theoretical arguments of this chapter are worked out in discussions of particular moral issues. We have already looked at truth and marriage. In the next chapter we will see how the theory illuminates the topic of **euthanasia.** Later we will look at some questions around the ownership of property, and other topics.

Rules are Required by Covenant and Creation

The doctrine of creation makes **rules** possible. It is because the world is ordered by God that we are able to discern clear patterns and regularities in nature. This provides the basis for modern science. It is a source of fascination that mathematical truths are so useful for describing the natural world in so many ways. Christians attribute this to the creative ordering work of God. It is possible to envisage modern science without Christian faith, of course. But, as we have already noted, belief in God's created order also extends to human life and behaviour. Here there is a different kind of complexity, and the crucial difference that humans do not conform automatically to God's purposes, but have the task of thinking them out.

It is because of God's creation and purpose that one marriage is in significant ways·like any other marriage. This makes a moral understanding of marriage both possible and necessary. To put this point negatively, we can say that human goodnesses and possibilities for human fulfilment are not infinitely variable. There are limits within which human beings achieve good ends. The emphasis on creation is only one way of establishing such limits. (For instance, a concern merely not to harm other people in the pursuit of happiness will also result in some moral limits, though these may possibly be more flexible than creation based limits.) The point about the connection of creation and morality is that it makes sense. Morality is firmly based on objective realities, not merely a matter of human construction, not based on human will, emotion or desires.

The creation rationale for moral rules is decisively reinforced by a covenant rationale. Covenant love means a faithful enduring reliable love. Covenant love is happy to commit itself, to bind itself with firm promises for the future. Such commitments, it should be noted, do not lead to a real loss of freedom. Rather, there is a freedom to be found within commitment. The unwillingness to make a commitment and stick to it is itself the denial of certain possibilities. The willingness to commit myself to my neighbour's good in a variety of ways provides an essential underpinning for many areas of morality. It has implications for every area of human life, including truth-telling, marriage, medicine, politics, economics and so on. In politics, a covenant ethic leads not only to justice, but also to certain strong emphases in our view of justice. It will lead to a concern for substantive as well as procedural justice. In the economic sphere, it will obviously mean honesty and fair-dealing, and it will also include a substantial concern for the welfare of the poor and vulnerable.

Covenant and creation thus provide a strong and clearly reasoned basis for strong moral rules. They also undergird two or three commonly advanced arguments for moral rules. Rules are important because of the moral frailty of human beings. They help to remind us of our duty when we are tempted by other opportunities. The rule that tells us to keep our promise serves to reinforce our resolve when it might be convenient to break it. Moral rules are also important in moral education. We teach our children 'Never tell a lie' even if we believe that there may be rare occasions when the truth should be concealed. Additionally, rules of all sorts, as well as legislation, are essential for social well-being. Any civilised society depends on a range of assumptions and commitments, some written, some spoken, some merely assumed. People need to be able to depend on one another in a great variety of ways, both morally and in custom and practice.

Within the framework of Christian belief in the love of God, in the creation of the world, and God's plan to redeem humanity from evil and suffering, Christian ethics is much less arbitrary than many versions of secular ethics. For secular ethics sees moral values as merely assigned by human purpose and will. Such values are changeable, and they may be fairly easily sacrificed when the pressure is on. One of the reasons why Christian morals are seen as restrictive is that they are always reluctant to give up any moral value, even when doing so seems the most convenient course of action. This is why traditional Christian ethics has always insisted on some strong moral prohibitions. Prohibitions protect the good-nesses of human life, truth, property and so on. They only seem arbitrary when their origin in the will of God is separated from his intelligent ordering of the world. Moral restrictions can appear oppressive if presented as mere demands, without a grasp of their rationale. If moral principles stand alone, and are not re-thought in new contexts and situations, then they can too easily become arbitrary and legalistic.

Covenant ethics underwrites all these reasons for thinking firm moral rules to be both right and desirable. But what do we mean by 'firm' moral rules? This question is not wholly straightforward and obvious, as some claim. But nor is it impossible, as others would have us think. We must now try to clarify it as carefully as we can.

The Meaning of Rules

It is easy to think of rather general principles that will always apply. Principles like 'Always be faithful in marriage to your spouse' or 'Always respect human life' are not empty principles. But they do not give answers to the harder questions. Does faithfulness to marriage imply that we should invariably resist divorce? Respect for life may easily lead to more than one conclusion about euthanasia. We need if possible to find more specific rules which will give more detailed guidance for specific questions.

On the other hand, it is not easy to find specific rules which do not have exceptions. 'Always tell the whole truth' and 'Never admit the possibility of divorce under any circumstances' simply do not do justice to the variety of human lives and circumstances. A covenant ethic is concerned to find reliable rules which will express in some areas the shape of reliable Christian love. The task is to find accurate prohibitions which describe the things which love will never do, and commands which describe ways in which it will always behave.

Our discussion of truth-telling can show us the way forward. In searching for the right formulation of a specific rule to enshrine respect for the truth, we went back to the purposes human speech is meant to achieve. The prohibition 'Never withhold the truth from one to whom it is due' expresses the central purpose, that of respecting and communicating the truth, but also includes recognition of the fact that truth-telling belongs within relationships. It is important to notice that this does not create exceptions to the rule. The rule 'Never withhold the truth from one to whom it is due' applies to all our speaking and communicating. The existence of occasions when the truth is not due from one person to another does not mean that the rule fails to apply on those occasions.

The application of moral rules always presupposes sufficient understanding of their meaning. When we use any moral rule, we need sufficient understanding to apply it to particular circumstances. It is not worth the trouble (nor possible in any case), to define a rule so carefully that it will exclude the opportunity for quibbling or misunderstanding. It has to be understood, for instance, that the truth is due to anyone; whether they are friend or stranger makes no difference to their right to the truth, in principle. The degree of their friendship will, of course make a difference to their right to my own personal knowledge. I owe it to anyone to tell them the time, if I know it; but I may choose who I tell what I am thinking about. If we have reason to question a particular rule, we may need to work out afresh what the themes of creation and covenant mean in new situations.

Of course there are all sorts of moral rule, from firm, exceptionless rules to general principles, maxims, and moral guidance. That a principle is not specific does not lessen its claim on us. The moral command that we should share with the poor and care for the needy cannot prescribe how much we should do in any given circumstance. Or again, it is not possible to define in advance exactly what justice will mean in new political circumstances, though it is certainly possible to define forms of injustice.

However, the question of what a moral rule actually means is not as obvious as it may sound. In order to see why so much care is sometimes needed in formulating and applying moral rules, we need to look for a moment at the complicated question of describing human action.

Moral Description of Action[1]

Giving an action its correct description is very close to formulating moral rules accurately. To call a particular action **murder** is to say that this was a wrongful killing. Formulating the rule which will describe what killings are to be called murder is to approach the same issue from the other direction. We must briefly examine the question from both directions.

---

[1] Cf. David Attwood, *Paul Ramsey's Political Ethics*, pp. 91–6.

The same action can be described in a great variety of ways:

1.   I pulled the trigger
2.   I fired the gun at him
3.   I killed a man.
4.   I murdered my enemy
5.   I took my revenge for his betrayal.
6.   I gave him his true deserts.

Each of these statements, which could all be made of the same event, tell us something different, or make a different moral claim about it. The first tells little except that it was my hand on the gun. It could have been an accident. The second tells us that I was aiming at him, and the third that I killed him. Both would seem to imply that there was an element of deliberation, though neither tell us exactly what was intended or what my motive may have been. The fourth is quite different, because it places my action as a deliberate and unjustified killing. The fifth tells us something of my motives, as does the sixth. The last one may be trying to construct some justification for an admittedly illegal act.

This highly simplified sequence of descriptions of the same action (all of which could be true at the same time) draw our attention to some of the complexities of providing a description of a relatively simple event which tells us all the morally relevant features. Was my action deliberate or accidental? Did I intend to kill him? Was there any legal justification for my action? Or moral justification? What, in other words, was my motive?

The decision as to whether this was an unjustified killing or not, and if it was, in what kind of way it was unjustified, has to be made before the action can be accurately described. 'I killed him but it was an accident' does not tell us enough. It could have been an accident for which I cannot be blamed (he had loaded the gun but assured me it was empty), or one which my forethought should certainly have prevented (I should not have been taking pot shots in an area where I knew people might suddenly appear). If it was a preventable accident, for which I am to blame, then this was unjustified killing, but since I did not deliberately intend his death it is not to be called murder.

Let us take another example, that of killing in warfare. Suppose that I am a soldier fighting in a war which I have no good reason to think is unjust. In this circumstance, my killing of an enemy soldier is intended to protect my own life and the lives of my friends. To decide whether this is a justified killing we need to have come to an analysis of the ethics of war, and see how that applies to this particular instance. Only then can we describe this action as justified or not. If we employ Just War terminology, we will find ourselves using words like 'discriminate', 'proportionate', and so on. These are words that are defined in particular ways to make distinctions between acts of war, and to point to morally relevant features.

This brief examination of the task of moral description has shown several key things. Human action is complex, and we need to know about the actor's intention and motivation. We may also need to know about the relevant circumstances, to see what explanation or justification they may offer. Before we come to any moral judgement of a particular killing there is a lot more we may need to know about. We might need to know not only the immediate circumstances, but also the full historical background. We may need to know about the character of the killer. It may be relevant to know about his mental state, and whether there are any extenuating circumstances which must influence our moral judgement. In all this we are wise to keep in mind that we can never arrive at a final moral verdict on anyone. The purpose of our moral discussion is for our learning, not to judge others.

In choosing the right words to describe an action, we need a good analysis of the ethics of the subject area, and then we will need to use the most helpful and accurate words of moral description derived from our moral analysis. Moral description of action thus may involve working backwards and forwards, as it were, between our basic principles and the circumstances of the event in question. As we can see, this task is very similar to the task of framing moral rules.

In order to reach an understanding of the moral legitimacy of taking human life, and to frame rules about it, we need to undertake a good deal of study about different cases. We clearly need moral rules about killing in warfare, and about capital punishment. We also need rules about **suicide**, and about **euthanasia**. We need to think about

abortion and **infanticide**. None of these topics can be handled adequately without considerable care about the language used, and the way our words apply to different cases.

The work of detailed examination of different types of cases is called **casuistry**. Casuistry has often been labelled as a very doubtful procedure — trying to find irrelevant or needlessly complex justification for morally doubtful behaviour. In fact casuistry is an important moral task. In the next chapter, in looking at euthanasia, we will examine an important topic where it is essential to be clear about the words and phrases we use. The basic aim is to ensure that the language used does justice at one and the same time both to the moral demands of love and to the detailed complexities that we actually encounter. What does covenant love — faithful care — actually mean when it comes to caring for the dying? Is there a way of expressing this meaning that is sufficiently specific to be helpful, but not so specific that it is accurate for only some cases and not others?

Human lives and human situations can be very complicated. It is no part of moral theory to reduce this complexity to make it fit preconceived formulae or rules. Rules can only be helpful when they accurately embody and define real similarities from one person to another, from one situation to another. That this is possible at all we owe to the order and pattern in God's creation. That it is sometimes very difficult, and sometimes quite inappropriate, we owe to the great variety of the world and of human life as God made it.

Avoiding Moralism and Legalism

The **legalist** is someone who stands or falls by keeping the letter of the moral law. Laws are applied rigidly, without attempting to interpret them to meet new cases. What matters is the keeping of the law, to the exclusion of other considerations like achieving good, or becoming a better person, because those things are interpreted only in terms of moral rules. The word 'moralist' is not so pejorative in tone. It usually refers to someone making detailed moral applications. Sometimes these can be helpful, sometimes they are irksome! For instance, an ecologically minded moralist will say things like 'You shouldn't waste so much water', advice which might or might not be morally accurate. (I might be running the tap in order to reduce the risk of drinking lead-polluted water.) The danger which both the moralist and the legalist share is that they take moral rules or moral advice out of context.

The point that the legalist overlooks is that moral rules are not themselves the essence or foundation of morality. Even the most fundamental and important moral commands (not to steal, not to kill, not to deceive) have a rationale on which they rest. The rationale has to do with our duty to love our neighbour, to conform our lives to God's purposes, to respect the God-given structures of life, truth, property and so on. Of course, virtually always, we respect the value God has placed on human life by not killing another human being. But it is a possibility, although paradoxical, that sometimes we protect human life by actually taking someone's life. This is the point of Genesis 9:6 'Whoever sheds the blood of a human, by a human shall that person's blood be shed; for in his own image God made human-kind.' Whether or not we should apply the saying in our day to warrant capital punishment is debated, but the verse supports the command-ment 'You shall not kill', as well as explaining when and why human life should be taken.

The insights of the moralist, or preacher, can be more helpful. But moralising can take all sorts of forms. Moralising is surely at its most helpful when it helps us to understand why keeping the moral rules is good for us, and when it gives us insight into ourselves and into human life. It is much less helpful, and we most resent it, when it either simply repeats what we already know, or when it has failed to make sufficient connections. The person who tells me I should use less water when I am simply clearing the pipes has missed the point. So has the person who tells me to use less water because there are people in Africa who have no piped water. The one who explains to me that my obsession with an emerald green lawn in the hottest summer contributes to the drying up of the local river puts it properly in context.

Both moralist and legalist, when they get it wrong, make essentially the same mistake. The mistake is in abstracting moral rules or moral advice from their proper context. The meaning of morality springs from wider beliefs in the nature of God, in the importance of love, in the good order and purposes of God's creation. It is on these wider truths that moral truths depend. That does not mean that we must always specifically refer back to them in a pedantic fashion. But if we take the moral commands as the fundamentals, then we are in danger.

The Contexts of Moral Thought

Moral rules have their meaning within a certain context of beliefs — beliefs about the purposes God has for human life. But morality is not just about individual actions — particular moments of decision. Keeping all the moral rules does not make someone into a person of good character, though someone of good character tends to keep moral rules. The truthfulness of a human being is more a matter of practice and habit than a series of decisions at unrelated moments. Our overall moral concern is to be people of the truth. There isn't any other way in which we can reflect the truthfulness of God. But to be a truthful person means actually telling the truth on particular occasions. The habit includes critical events which can test our real strength of character.

The moral judgements we make cannot overlook the histories of the people involved, and the events and circumstances that lie in the background. Too exclusive a concentration on an isolated incident can lead to the mistake of the legalist, that of applying moral rules out of context. Of course not all circumstances are relevant — sometimes they are, sometimes they aren't. For instance, the circumstances of conception (whether it was rape), may be relevant to the question of abortion. From some points of view, too, there may be all sorts of extenuating circumstance which must be taken into account in some sense. Perhaps, at times, they should make no substantial difference to what ought to be done. Someone's compulsive adultery may perhaps be better understood in the light of childhood events and relationships. But it does not alter a negative verdict on the adultery itself. But even this does not say that repentance can always be instantaneous. A decision to reform may still take quite a time to carry through, in order to complete as well as may be any disentangling of old relationships and commitments.

In this discussion we come to the boundary between those who deal with individuals, and those who try to form more general principles. The place of general principles is far from the whole of morality. The pastor, the novelist and the dramatist are just as much dealing with morality as the moral theologian or philosopher.

Finally, we must remember that it is no human task to pass final moral judgements on one another. The point of moral thought is to help us think more clearly about what we should do, and how we should live; in other words, the future not the past. So we cannot escape the importance of considering types of action, types of situations. At the same time, there is something provisional about all our moral discernments.

In the account of morality we are describing, morality is dependent on faith. That leads to the slightly counter-intuitive idea that moral truth is no more certain than faith. Just as the truths of faith will only be fully understood in God's kingdom, so also moral truth cannot be perfectly understood here and now. Our grasp of truth, love, and the purposes of God is only provisional. We do not know the fullness of love or truth, or other virtues, yet. We can perhaps be more confident about some negative things — what is unloving, unjust, untrue. In a similar way it is often easier to say what faith does not mean — what God is not like, rather than to say exactly what he is.

There is a perfectionist strand in the New Testament, perhaps most notably in the sayings of Jesus. 'Be perfect, therefore, as your heavenly Father is perfect' (Matt. 5:48). That this is not an add-on extra will already be clear from the themes of covenant and creation. We cannot be satisfied with less than a complete fulfilment of God's design for us. However, the setting of the command to perfection is also clear enough in the New Testament (e.g. Matt. chapter 5, and 1 John 3). We will not achieve perfection before the final coming of God's kingdom. The ideal certainly makes its call on us already, but we cannot realistically expect to attain it yet.

There is, then, a certain provisionality in all our moral actions, even in our very best. Again, we must remind ourselves that our moral shortcomings, which we cannot wholly escape, do not say the final or decisive word about our lives. The New Testament repeatedly makes clear that the crucial element of judgement is our relationship to Christ — are we those who believe in Christ, who have eternal life in him, who are justified by faith in him, who are 'in Christ'? God's plan of reconciliation and redemption means bringing those who have rebelled against God back into union with him. As Paul is at pains to make clear, this does not mean that God releases us from his moral claim. Our moral renewal takes its starting point from our free forgiveness. **Forgiveness**, which in some ways is such a puzzle for morality, must be at the heart of Christian morality, and we will return to it in a later chapter.

In the meantime, this chapter has tried to sketch an overall picture of what moral discernment is aiming at. It has inevitably needed to be fairly abstract. In considering euthanasia, in the next chapter, we will examine how this works out in a difficult and controversial area. We will see that our structure of moral thought does indeed enable us to relate clear moral perceptions accurately and helpfully to genuinely difficult human decisions.

Nine

Euthanasia

The aim of this chapter is to show how the ideas we have considered so far help us understand the nature of confusing moral questions. The themes of creation and covenant, and the way they take shape in principles and rules, illuminate the difficult questions that can arise at the end of someone's life. At the same time the practical question of caring for the dying will help to clarify and explain the theoretical framework for ethics. In all ethical discussions, there is a two-way traffic between principles and practicalities. The principles are designed to help us understand practical problems, but new cases and situations also make us think afresh about the principles and lead us to grasp them more deeply.

Two words of caution are essential at the beginning of any chapter of this kind. Clearly, first, it is not possible to answer all questions or meet all alternative points of view in a discussion of euthanasia as short as this. Our claim, rather, is that the approach we will take is itself a serious one — that is, it does not intend to foreshorten serious discussion or simplify complicated issues. In most introductions to academic subjects (whether in schools, colleges or in books) a measure of simplification is both essential and acceptable. But in moral matters it is not usually acceptable, because we know the real complexities and confusions in our own lives. The second word of caution follows. In this chapter all we aim to do (and all that the moralist can ever aim to do), is to clarify where the practical difficulties lie. I do not think, for instance, that all the difficult cases of euthanasia can actually be answered by the moralist, so that it is possible to say (even if all the facts were known) that such and such a course of action is definitely the right one. Perhaps this is also true for medical staff in individual cases. But more generally, the moralist cannot make a medical diagnosis, or even say what kind of diagnosis is possible. Many aspects of caring for the dying are matters of medical skill. Our moral understanding has to respect this skill in such a way that medical insight helps to form our moral principles. This means also that moral principles cannot actually tell us specifically what to do in caring for individual people. In some areas of morality it is only a short step from the moral principle to the action. It is not a problem to know what 'no stealing' means when paying for a meal in a restaurant. But in caring for people at the end of their lives there is a much bigger gap between 'no killing' and deciding on the right course of treatment.

Before considering one or two specific case-studies, we will first consider what creation and covenant mean in caring for the dying. Then, working between the theological framework and the case studies, we will see how specific moral rules can help to define the moral framework within which medical care operates.[1] It needs also to be noted that this chapter is directed primarily towards reaching a moral understanding, rather than an argument about legislation.

Creation, Life and Death

The creation of human beings is the pinnacle of God's work in Genesis chapter one. 'God made man in his own image'. In chapter two, the creation of man and woman is described in a different way, but there is no mistaking the account of God's special interest in human life. God gives the man his breath, the breath of life. It is not clear whether God intended human beings to live for ever, but after they disobey his command and eat the forbidden fruit they are banished from the garden before they can eat from the tree of life. It is assumed throughout the Bible that life is the gift of God. Human beings are not to kill each other, because they are made in the image of God. The protection of life is so important that, paradoxically, the life of a

---

[1] The understanding considered here owes much to the work of the Linacre Centre and those working with it. See *Euthanasia and Clinical Practice: trends, principles and alternatives*, A Working Party Report, Linacre Centre. This is helpfully reprinted in *Euthanasia, Clinical Practice and the Law*, (ed.) Luke Gormally.

murderer is to be taken. 'Whoever sheds the blood of a man, by man shall his blood be shed, for man was made in the image of God' (Gen. 9.6).

Just as life is a gift of God, so is the **death** of every human being appointed by God. The Psalms contain many moving meditations on the shortness of human life. The 'three score years and ten' comes from the Psalms, and so does the saying much used at funerals: 'the days of man are but as grass: he flourishes like a flower of the field'. Death is inevitable. 'God means to kill us all in the end, and one day he will succeed' says the twentieth century cynic. But though the Bible knows the reality of death, it continues to see death as an enemy. 'The last enemy to be defeated will be death' (1 Cor. 15:26). Jesus, in his resurrection, has overcome the power of death. From then on, death is not the end. But the knowledge of a life beyond the grave does not make death a friend, but an enemy still to be overcome.

The knowledge that God appoints death for us all, and that death is not the end, lends a certain ambivalence to our struggles against sickness and death. On one hand, the Christian loves and cherishes life, as the gift of God, as the first gift which makes all God's other gifts possible. On the other hand, the fact that earthly life is seen in the light of a better life to come means that a certain measure of acceptance of death is possible. But this acceptance is never really a welcome. Even John Donne, who had as lively a preoccupation with death and heaven as any Christian, knew this. In one place he compares human lives to pages in a book: 'All mankind is of one Author, and is one volume; when one man dies, one chapter is not torn out of the book, but translated into a better language; and every chapter must be so translated'. A little later comes the famous passage: 'Any man's death diminishes me, because I am involved in mankind; and therefore never send to know for whom the bell tolls; it tolls for thee'.[2] Death is a diminution indeed.

Christian ambivalence about death provides the context for care of the dying. Sometimes medical care towards the end of some people's lives needs to recognise this. Perhaps sometimes medical care can give up too easily, and welcome death too quickly as bringing an end to life's pain and miseries. More often it seems

---

[2] Meditation 17, in *Selected Prose*, pp. 125–6.

that the inevitability of death is not admitted, as if someone near the end of life need to keep fighting every new complication. One sometimes wonders if the powerful medical technologies now available are somehow felt to give power over death itself. Of course they cannot postpone death indefinitely, and no one would dream of denying that. But perhaps the attempts which are sometimes made to preserve life stem from a failure fully to come to terms with the inevitability of death, combined with the lack of belief in a life which transcends death. For if this life is all that there is, there is no point at which death can truly be accepted.

Covenant Love and the Protection of Life

It is clear that love requires us not to murder another human being. 'Thou shalt not kill' is best understood as a prohibition of murder rather than as a prohibition of all killing. The commandment belonged to a society where capital punishment was required; and where killing in battle was not questioned, but taken for granted. That love requires us not to kill is confirmed by Jesus when he speaks of love as the source of all the commands. This leaves us with two questions. First, how does Jesus, and the New Testament as a whole, understand the prohibition of killing? Second, what is the moral meaning of murder, or we might say, what constitutes the forbidden killing we call 'murder'? The answer to the first question will help with the second.

Jesus called attention to the point that it is not just actions which come under moral judgement, but words, thoughts and attitudes as well. He also widened the scope of the commandment when he insisted that the duty of love is owed to enemies as well as to friends. But the point here which is most relevant to the question of euthanasia is that which concentrates on our inner attitudes and motives. Anything which proceeds from hatred is morally equivalent to murder.

At this point we need to consider the difference between motive and intention. When euthanasia takes place in order deliberately to shorten someone's dying, it is important to be clear about the meaning of the words **motive** and **intention**, which have a technical meaning in discussions of this kind.[3] It is possible to intend someone's death with the best of motives, if those motives are to spare someone needless suffering and pain. When someone is deliberately killed, then the intention is to cause death; but the motive is to relieve suffering. The argument of those who support euthanasia is that the intention directly to end someone's life may be justified by love for the patient, especially if the patient wants to end their life. The Christian tradition, and the law, has never accepted this argument. Instead, any intention to end someone's life has been held morally and legally forbidden.

A number of reasons have been given for saying that one should never intend another person's death. Some of them have been intended to protect the sanctity, or dignity, or value, of human life. Intentions are something which the law can deal with (admittedly with difficulty), but the law does not take motives into account when determining guilt. Weakening the prohibition of direct killing may leave a large loophole in the law which could be exploited in all sorts of ways. These and other arguments have to do with the role of the law in protecting society, in restraining those with evil intentions and motives. But such arguments do not resolve the question as to whether it could be morally right ever to bring about someone's death in order to end their suffering. The reason this has never been accepted has to do with the nature of God's gift of life. The meaning of love has to be understood within our knowledge of God's created purposes. To intend anyone's death, and then directly to bring it about, is to usurp God's gift.

The fact that both intention and motive have to respect the gift of life, and express our love for one another, only brings us to the beginning of the question of euthanasia. For when someone is dying, it is not always straightforward to see how our ambivalence about death is to be worked out. How shall we embody our respect for life, while still recognising the final inevitability of death? To tackle this we will look at some fictional case studies. Obviously this can only suggest possible answers for some circumstances; it is not possible to consider everything!

---

[3] It is often unnecessary to try to distinguish motive from intention, but this is one area where we need to. But it has to be said that it can still be a very confusing distinction!

Case Study 1: Painful Terminal Illness

For many people the fear of dying is closely coupled with the fear of pain. There are too many stories from those who have seen close friends and relatives dying in great pain and discomfort for these fears to be easily set at rest. It is this which gives the word **cancer** much of its dread, so that it is a word many find uneasy to voice. Why then not bring someone's life to a merciful end, rather than let them die in fear and pain? The original Greek derivation of the word 'euthanasia' is a 'good death'. Why should people not have the moral right to seek a good death rather than a bad one?

The fears are real enough, but fortunately the facts do not give grounds for all the fears which many people feel. Cancer is a serious illness, but of course it is by no means always fatal. A large proportion of cancer sufferers can be treated and make a good recovery. We need to be careful not to exaggerate the fearfulness of the disease. Cancer can be a terminal illness, however, and that is our concern here. But pain in any terminal illness can usually be relieved and controlled to a quite acceptable level. Only a very few patients need experience pain (less than five percent). Morphine, or other analgesics (pain-relieving drugs) can be used to keep the vast majority of patients free from pain. The widespread fear of a lingering painful death is quite misplaced. For instance, Dr Robert Twycross, a leading authority in this field, makes the point that a leading advocate of euthanasia in the Netherlands agrees that euthanasia is rarely or never called for to prevent a painful death.[4]

But doesn't the administration of pain relief shorten life, and if so, is this not a form of euthanasia? The answer to this, on both medical and moral grounds, is 'No'. The proper use of analgesics to relieve pain, so far from shortening life, may well have the opposite effect. When a patient is free from pain, and sleep is better, that is a positive factor.

> 'Contrary to popular belief, the correct use of morphine in the relief of cancer pain generally carries no greater risk of shortening life than the use of aspirin. Morphine given regularly every four hours by mouth, is a very safe drug provided the patient is not dying from exhaustion as a result of weeks or months

---

[4] For instance, in the CARE video *Living Dangerously*, 1992.

of intolerable pain associated with insomnia and poor nutrition. In fact the correct use of morphine is more likely to prolong a patient's life rather than to shorten it, because he is more rested and pain free. It is, of course, possible to use drugs that are generally safe in a dangerous (that is, more risky) way.'[5]

In the closing stages of life, however, the picture typically changes. A time may come when larger doses of analgesic are required in order to keep a patient free from pain, and this may hasten death. If the patient dies, foreseeably, as a result, is this the same as intending the patient's death? Advocates of euthanasia argue that there is no moral difference between pain relieving drugs which bring about death, and directly administering a lethal injection. Surely the intention in both cases is the same, they say. Therefore, they argue, it is simpler and more dignified to take control of death, when dying is inevitable. Again, there is a medical and a moral answer to this point. While the intention of the doctor is to relieve pain, even if death may ensue, the outcome is not necessarily predictable. The aim is to relieve pain, to sedate, to help the patient rest and sleep. This is the aim, the intention of the doctor. But even when the doctor can foresee death coming as a result, he need not directly intend the patient's death. Perhaps it is better to say that his action has two effects. The primarily intended effect is the relief of pain; but the side-effect is the increased risk of death.[6] Here the increased risk of death needs to be considered in relation to the nearness of death. When death is inevitable, shortening life by a few hours or days may be acceptable in order to prevent pain and distress.

The point made earlier about the impossibility of the moralist alone giving clear and easy answers is clear even in so apparently uncomplicated a scenario. In looking at the medical management of the dying of a terminally ill patient it is essential to bear in mind the impossibility of a complete diagnosis. The doctor does not know exactly how long a patient will live, or how he or she will respond to treatments. The effects of drugs cannot be known with precision. Doctor, patient and carers are also caught between life and death, on the balance between

---

[5] Gormally, *Euthanasia*, p. 79, citing a journal article by R.G. Twycross.

[6] In making this moral judgement, we must remember that there are different ways to describe an action from a moral point of view (cf. the discussion in Chapter 8). The claim I am making here is that we should regard the primary intention of the doctor (what is directly and chiefly aimed at) as the defining element in the description.

the desire to live and the acknowledgement of death's inevitability. As this balance shifts, the appropriate balance of treatment and desire also shifts, and rightly so.

Case Study 2: Incurable Degenerative Illnesses

Those who argue for euthanasia put forward other reasons for deliberately bringing life to an end. Pain is not the only reason to wish for death. There can be distressing symptoms, not so much painful as thoroughly unpleasant and humiliating. Patients with some illnesses are likely to degenerate, losing various physical or mental abilities and becoming progressively more dependent on others, and progressively less like the person they were when healthy and active. Some of these illnesses, though incurable, are not fatal, so that death may be a long time coming. Is there not a case, if a patient has clearly and repeatedly expressed the desire to die, but is unable to take their own life, for them to be helped to die under proper medical and legal supervision?

It will be clear enough that the line of reasoning we have so far followed about the sanctity of life and the sovereignty of God over human life will answer this question 'No'. It does not fall to human beings to determine to kill for these reasons. Fundamentally, it is wrong deliberately to take the life of any human being because this would be to usurp God's sovereignty. Respect for God, and his gift of life, is called for. The reasons we have briefly outlined apply to this kind of illness as well. Our responsibility is to show love and care within the circumstances of life. How someone lives, how they die — these are our concerns. To determine that they will die, that is not our task.

In one sense this is a sufficient answer. But it may be worthwhile to consider how this answer can be seen as a good one, even in the most distressing circumstances, and even from slightly different Christian points of view. For perhaps we ought to ask how an ethic of responsibility would answer this question.[7] Is there room in a slightly different ethical framework to give a different, and seemingly more

---

[7] As was discussed above in Chapter 7.

compassionate, answer? For an ethic stressing human responsibility will perhaps want to argue that God's sovereignty does not mean that human beings should put all responsibility for the dying process back to God.

There might be several ways to defend the prohibition of euthanasia, to show that the moral decision made is also a good one, in terms of overall responsibility and consequences. We will focus on two points, one mainly legal, and one mainly philosophical. From a legal point of view, it is vital that the law against murder admits no loopholes. From a philosophical point of view, one can ask what is meant by dignity in dying. The first discussion is I believe compelling both legally and morally. The second discussion attempts to widen our attitudes and ask if we are in danger of expecting too much in the medical and technical control of our physical lives.

There are great dangers in legalising killing. Even in Holland, where euthanasia is legally acceptable under certain circumstances, this effectively takes the form of an agreement not to prosecute, as Dutch Case Law has come to accept the defence of 'necessity'. The Dutch are of course aware of the danger of abuse, of the literal possibility of allowing someone to get away with murder. But the Dutch experience is not very encouraging. The guidelines appear to make clear that the patient must freely request euthanasia, and that this request must be 'well considered, durable and persistent'. Notwithstanding this, statistics gathered for the year 1990 show that in 1000 cases life was terminated by a doctor without an explicit request. This figure has to be compared with 2300 cases of voluntary euthanasia, and a much larger figures where doctors reported hastening death by the use of pain-killing drugs, or by withholding or withdrawing treatment.[8]

This experience adds great weight to the fear expressed by Dame Cicely Saunders, one of the pioneers of **hospice** care for the dying. She sometimes seems more ready than other opponents of euthanasia to concede that there may be very occasional cases where euthanasia seems to be the best course of action. But she then points out that if euthanasia is allowed, individual people may come under pressure to ask to die for the sake of sparing the feelings of

---

[8] Gormally (ed.), *Euthanasia*, p. 224. These are two numerical examples extracted from the table on that page.

relatives and others.[9] There are those who can all too easily feel themselves a burden; and it is the clear duty of those caring for them to assure them that they are not. The legalisation of euthanasia could make this much more difficult.

These arguments give good reasons for many doctors and lawyers to be unhappy about proposals to legalise euthanasia in Britain. A change in the law would make doctors responsible for ending the life of a patient, an action quite out of keeping with the concern to cure and heal. Nigel Cameron points out that it is an essential feature of the Hippocratic tradition in medicine that a sharp separation is made between curing and killing.[10] It need not be so: the medical power that exists at the end of life can as easily be used to determine life's end as to postpone or prevent it — to kill as well as to heal.

The legal caution about accepting voluntary euthanasia has to be considered very carefully. It is also worth thinking about what is meant by 'death with dignity'. The word dignity can mean a number of different things. For instance, the dignity of a dog or a horse leads us to treat it quite differently from the way we treat humans. If a horse breaks its leg, or a dog develops diabetes, it is quite an open question whether or not the animal should be killed. Whether or not they are treated, or put to sleep, is more a matter of circumstance and sentiment than of morality. If the animal is killed, that may well be seen as the most dignified option, rather than trying to preserve life in an impaired form. On the other hand, dignity for a human being means something quite different. True human dignity is not incompatible with weakness and need. 'The spirit of serene acknowledgement of the reality of one's needful situation (a spirit that could be called meekness) is much more real an expression of human dignity than any struggle to maintain a fiction of independence'.[11] At the same time, sickness and disability does involve real indignity. Being unable to work, or to walk, or to speak, are very real indignities, and there are many much worse than those. But we do not say that if such things make someone no longer capable of fulfilling their proper function in life, they should therefore be killed. Being paralysed, or speechless, or unable to work, are all

---

[9] E.g. in the CARE video *Living Dangerously*.
[10] *The New Medicine*, pp. 60–61.
[11] Gormally, *Euthanasia and Clinical Practice*, ch. 4, sec. 5.

indignities of different kinds. Human sickness and dying have an inevitably undignified element. There is therefore something essentially paradoxical in speaking about death with dignity.

This is not to say that considerations of dignity are irrelevant in caring for the sick or the dying. It is of course entirely right to do everything to protect and maintain the patient's dignity. If someone cannot walk, that should not and need not detract at all from the respect shown to them. One has to think a bit more carefully, and work a bit harder, to see how to minimise the patient's indignity and dependence. It may also be important to say that some indignities seem worse to the onlooker, or in prospect, than they actually are to the person affected. If you were to ask someone 'Could you manage without your right hand?' they would no doubt say 'No'. In fact they would learn to manage, as some people already do. Perhaps the question 'Would you rather die than suffer the indignity of . . . ?' may also be answered differently as a hypothetical than as a real question.

Here we return to our theological understanding of death. In Christian faith the approach of death is awaited with mixed feelings. The main thought is that life is precious; that it is the gift of God, never to be undervalued or let go of lightly. But the second thought is that death is not the end, because Jesus Christ was raised from death. Death is not the ultimate defeat. One way of putting this is to say that death is the enemy ('the last enemy' 1 Cor. 15); but a defeated enemy. I have heard Christians say that death is a 'friendly enemy', because it brings us one step closer to God. The idea of death with dignity needs to be fitted into this understanding of death. Death is to be resisted, and the fight for life comes before almost all other considerations. But finally death cannot be fought for ever, and at the point where it becomes an immediate prospect, the idea of fighting it fades and other concerns move to the foreground.

Case Study 3: Patients in a Permanent Vegetative State

The case of Tony Bland, whose treatment was finally considered by the House of Lords in 1993, brought the question of the so-called 'persistent vegetative state' (**PVS**) to the headlines. A PVS patient is in a persistent coma, permanently unconscious, and after a certain passage of time may be diagnosed as having no possibility of recovery and return to normal life and health. The brain activity of a PVS patient gives no indication of any awareness or sensation of any kind. Nevertheless the patient is able to breathe and may exhibit certain reflex reactions. The patient's life is sustained by artificial feeding through a tube; antibiotics may be administered in order to combat infections. In their judgement their Lordships gave permission for the withdrawal of feeding, which led inevitably to the death of the patient. However they insisted that such withdrawal of feeding could only take place with specific judicial agreement in each case.

How does our discussion of euthanasia bear upon the question of PVS? In the comments that follow, no attempt will be made to resolve the question of the right treatment of PVS patients. The aim is to explore how our moral understanding can be spelt out in this kind of case. It also serves as a reminder of the point that we cannot always know with precision and control what the right course of action actually is. To admit this does not invalidate the clear principle that we should never intend the death of another. It is not the principles that are called into question by borderline cases. Rather, the interpretation of the circumstances is what is difficult, as in the case of PVS.[12]

The first question that we have to ask is whether the patient is truly alive. We will assume that we are talking about a patient who has been diagnosed as having no prospect of recovery, a patient with no brain activity apart from those required to sustain breathing and other basic reflexes.[13] Is such a patient alive in the true sense of the word? This question asks us to consider if there is an analogy to other cases where the exact moment of death is very hard to determine. For instance, there might be an analogy with a patient who is only kept alive with artificial respiration, where there is no evidence of brain activity. Or perhaps there might be an analogy with the baby born anencephalic, where there is no brain and life cannot be sustained for long. In both of these cases, there is no obligation to maintain whatever physical

---

[12] It is more than a little surprising that the law lords appear to have allowed the legal principles to be altered by the circumstances of the Bland case. See John Keown 'Courting Euthanasia?: Tony Bland and the Law Lords'.

[13] The need for caution here is underlined by a report in The Guardian (16.3.96) of someone showing signs of recovery after seven years in unconsciousness.

signs of life there are, as there is no human life. Death has already taken place. As I understand it, the present judgment of the medical profession is that these analogies cannot safely be drawn in the case of PVS patients. It is not safe or accurate to say that death has (effectively) occurred. Even if this is suspected, the patient should be given the benefit of the doubt. Whichever way this medical discussion goes, it is a debate requiring a high degree of medical skill.

The second question asks what is the point of continued medical, that is therapeutic, treatment? The point of medical care is to restore a patient to health, at least to a point where some kind of normal functioning can take place. In the case of PVS patients, there are some patients where this has been judged impossible. Here, it seems that while nothing should be done deliberately to hasten death, it may not be medically appropriate to prevent dying should that happen in the normal course of events. This raises the question of what is to count as medical treatment.

At least three aspects of medical care are relatively routinely used with PVS patients. First the patient is in hospital, receiving 24-hour nursing attention. This includes, second, feeding by tube, since clearly the patient cannot be fed in any other way. Thirdly, many but not all patients need antibiotic treatment since they are relatively susceptible to infection. Considering these in reverse order, it is clear that administering antibiotics is medical treatment. In the circumstances described, medical treatment can be considered futile, since there is no prospect of a return to health. This leads to the question whether feeding by tube is a medical treatment, or part of the ordinary care owed to any living human being. There does not seem to be any straightforward way to adjudicate this particular question, which is disputed by doctors, moralists and others. On the one hand, feeding is a normal obligation when caring for someone unable to feed themselves, and starving a PVS patient to death would seem perhaps a rather undignified procedure (though we are assuming that they can have no sense that this is happening). On the other hand, feeding someone by tube is not a normal method of feeding; withdrawing nourishment by tube can hardly be equated with failing to spoon feed someone unable to feed themselves. Nor is it (perhaps) right to say that this is starving the patient; all one is doing is withdrawing medical treatment and letting nature take its course. Finally, what about continuous nursing care in hospital? It may perhaps be asked whether the family or other carers might not take the patient home, and do the best they can to care for the patient at home, say with daily visits from medical staff. If this leads to a decline in the patient's ability to sustain life, perhaps that is appropriate.

There can be no open-and-shut answers to all medical questions. The tentative discussion of the treatment of PVS patients makes this clear. Is the patient alive? What treatment is appropriate? Is feeding to be called treatment, or everyday care? We cannot find safe or conclusive answers to these extremely hard questions.

Does this invalidate our overall analysis of the ethics of euthanasia? So far from invalidating it, it reveals its worth. Even here our approach has two particular merits. The first is that it directs our attention to certain questions, and these are questions which go to the heart of the issue. The questions to be pursued are those relating to the condition of the patient, the accurate description of that condition, the prognosis and so on. They also lead us to ask about appropriate forms of care. The second merit is precisely that we are warned to tread carefully because we do not have all the answers. We have some confidence, but this remains limited, and in a certain way, provisional.

Covenant Ethics or Value Ethics

Euthanasia offers us the chance briefly to compare the different ways in which an ethic based on values compares with a creation–covenant ethic. The essential difference is that covenant ethics offer a structured way of understanding the issues, while values offer only a series of preferences.[14]

Value language begins with the value of human life. The value assigned to human life may be derived from Christian assumptions, or from other views (including other religions, or humanism, etc.) The value of the patient's life is the first thing to be considered. Other

---

[14] Of course it is possible to use the language of values as a way of presenting arguments and conclusions derived on other grounds. Not all talk of values need follow the underlying logic which belongs best with the word 'value'.

values and disvalues then need to be considered. These include the value of compassion, and the disvalues of pain, incapacity and indignity. One has to include also the values of dignity, and autonomy. After considering the values that immediately concern the dying patient and those directly caring, we must then think of the general consequences for others of what is done to this one person. This leads us to further values to be considered; in particular the welfare of other sick and incapacitated people, the dying and others.

It quickly becomes clear that we have a choice of moral method. We can either assert the importance of one or two values in relation to the others, or we can begin to trace the interrelationships between them. If we take the latter course, then we may reach a point where we simply weigh some values as more significant than others, or perhaps we may go on to try to reach a reasoned conclusion.[15] In order to do that, we need some reasoned moral principles, some method of arguing, and some way to conclude argument. We have, in other words, to translate 'values' back into substantial moral arguments. The language of values, which we thought would provide a way in which we could arbitrate between differing moral arguments, cannot do what we hoped. Moreover, it opens up the very real prospect of reducing all moral discussion to a simple comparison of moral preferences.

Conclusion

The three case studies can only illustrate in a rather general way how the moral framework we have begun to develop can help to illuminate an area of medical ethics. Our concern has been to see that a view of death within Christian faith makes sense of the narrow path that has to be found. On one side lies the aggressive approach which seems to regard every death as a medical failure; on the other side is either too easy an acceptance of death, or a wish to bring death under control by determining its time and manner. The first fails to appreciate that

---

[15] For a sensitive and subtle argument about euthanasia which builds a substantial argument using the values of autonomy, the patient's best interests, and the sanctity of life, see Ronald Dworkin *Life's Dominion: An Argument about Abortion and Euthanasia*, ch. 7, 'Dying and Living'. I need hardly add that I disagree with Dworkin's method and with his conclusions.

death is within God's sovereignty, a gift that is only for a time; the latter that God's gift is too precious, too sacred, for us ever to reject it, whether for ourselves or for someone else.

This perspective, it has become clear, does not provide all the understanding which can only belong to a full moral–medical skill. But our claim is that any attempt to care for the dying which does not come to terms with such a perspective is much more likely to miss the path. Furthermore, our perspective does provide a strong principle which clearly and definitely prohibits some sorts of action (deliberate ending of life), even while recognising that in some circumstances even such a rule may need very careful interpretation.

Our aim is to explore a Christian ethic. But we should ask how relevant this is in a society whose ethos runs more and more counter to this ethic.[16] While it may be true that our society is impatient with language about the sovereignty of God, it is also true that our society is deeply concerned about the worth of individual life. The word 'worth' here is not identical to the word 'sanctity', but it is perhaps not far from it. Our view of the worth of human life, and the importance of individual rights, also owes a very great deal to the Christian tradition and the Christian ethic. Such an understanding is still very important to our legal system, perhaps most obviously in laws concerning homicide. Other elements too of the approach we have followed may very well find echoes in secular society.

---

[16] We will look more fully at this question in Chapter 13.

Ten

The Demand for Perfection

In a saying placed by Matthew at the heart of the Sermon on the Mount, Jesus says: 'Be perfect, therefore, as your heavenly Father is perfect'. The saying comes at the end of the chapter in which Jesus intensifies all moral commands. We are to love our enemies, as well as our friends; we are not to be angry or even rude, just as much as not murdering; we are to avoid adultery, but we are to avoid looking with lust as well. What did Jesus mean by commanding us to be perfect? Surely he was aware that these standards are simply unrealistic?

In order to put the apparently impossible ethic taught by Jesus into its context, we need to make the connections he made with the kingdom of God, and the perfection of God. There are several ways to bring out the importance of this context for moral thought. Most obviously, (1) we can look more carefully at the moral teaching of Jesus himself, to examine the style of his teaching and see if we can discover more precisely what he meant by the command to be perfect. We can also try to see (2) how a Kingdom ethic fits with the ethics of creation and covenant love that we have examined so far. We will see (3) that one of the ways in which an ethic of the Kingdom refocuses our attention is that it concentrates on the kind of people we are meant to be. Ethics is not just about moral rules which regulate separate actions. One theologian who has made this point with great insistence and insight is Stanley Hauerwas, and we will consider one or two of his themes. Finally (4) we will see how looking at morality from the viewpoint of the Kingdom affects our sense of what morality actually is. On the whole we assume that we simply know what it means to say that something is right to do. But if moral knowledge is only really known in so far as we know God, and his perfection, then our moral knowledge is perhaps less secure than we had assumed. In all these discussions, we will keep Jesus' saying in mind: 'Be perfect, therefore, as your heavenly Father is perfect'.

1. Jesus' Moral Teaching[1]

It is often said that the heart of Christian morality is to be found in the Sermon on the Mount. What is perhaps less often noticed is that the Sermon on the Mount gives a very different setting for morality from that in the Ten Commandments. While the Commandments typically look back to the acts of God in the past, Jesus looks forward to the perfection of God's Kingdom. The meaning and the motive of morality is not so much what God has done for us, as what he wants to do with us. For instance 'Blessed are the pure in heart, for they will see God'. And Jesus makes it clear that total purity is indeed required. Nothing less than perfection will do (the persistent thought of Matthew 5, and throughout Jesus' teaching).

There are two sayings about the eye in the Sermon on the Mount, which bring us quickly to the heartbeat of Jesus' moral teaching. 'If your right eye causes you to sin, take it out and throw it away! It is much better for you to lose a part of your body than to have your whole body thrown into hell' (5:29). 'The eyes are like a lamp for the body. If your eyes are sound, your whole body will be full of light; but if your eyes are no good, your body will be in darkness. So if the light in you is darkness, how terribly dark it will be!' (6:22–23). It is not often noticed by Bible commentaries that these two sayings are complementary. Both come at the midpoint of the section to which they belong. Like the opening and closing verses of each section, they help to crystallise the main point being made. The section running from Matthew 5:17–48 is about moral perfection, the completeness of God's demand on us, and the vital importance of rooting evil out of our lives. In order to do this, it may be necessary to take drastic action to remove

---

[1] There is a vast wealth of literature on this subject. One of the most helpful books is A.E. Harvey, *Strenuous Commands: The Ethic of Jesus*.

causes of temptation and sin — 'Tear out your eyes'. The section from Matthew 6:1–7:11, which follows immediately, turns to teach us about our need to look to God in prayer, to receive the rewards and the good things he wants to give us. There is a repeated reference to the reward God will give us, and the section ends 'How much more, then, will your Father in heaven give good things to those who ask him' (7:11). The saying about the good eye, giving light to the body, is at the middle of the section and acts as an illustration of the whole. If we take the two sayings together, the point is clear. If we wish to live pure lives, to the standard of God's perfection, then our attention must be wholly fixed on God.

Harvey's study of the ethics of Jesus argues that the words of Jesus are best seen as proverbs and maxims which are often deliberately one-sided or exaggerated in order to make a point. They aim to jolt the listener out of complacency, provoking fresh thought, new perspectives and reordered priorities. A proverb does not give both sides of the argument. Instead, it makes a particular point with energy and exaggeration, aiming to get under our skin, to make us think again. Proverbs 10:21 claims 'Fools die for lack of sense'. There may be a sting in the saying: 'Like vinegar to the teeth, and smoke to the eyes, so are the lazy to their employers' (10:26). Often a point is made with humour or satire: 'Like a gold ring in a pig's snout is a beautiful woman without good sense' (11.22). All these qualities are found in Jesus' sayings.

Of course, there is a marked contrast between the main message of Proverbs and the central teaching of Jesus. The wisdom of Proverbs is worldly, emphasising the earthly rewards of uprightness, good sense and virtue. Jesus, on the other hand, stresses a heavenly reward, thinking how we must consider what is best for us in the light of heaven. Jesus wanted his followers to be more completely aware of the reality and perfect purity of God. A new perspective is given to everyday life by the knowledge that the Kingdom of God is our true home. But this sharp contrast need not blind us to way in which Jesus is just like the teacher of wisdom. Proverbs assumes that we want to do well in this life, in the long run, while Jesus urges us to do well in heaven. Because we are so preoccupied with the things of this world, Jesus uses every method to make us look at life from a different perspective.

This means, for instance, not that wealth is wrong, but that it is irrelevant. Its danger lies in its powerful tendency to draw our attention. In attending so anxiously to the irrelevant and transient business of money, we are thereby distracted and prevented from looking to God. The main point is made by Matthew 6:19–21 'Do not store up riches for yourselves here on earth, where moths and rust destroy, and robbers break in and steal. Instead, store up riches for yourselves in heaven, where moths and rust cannot destroy, and robbers cannot break in and steal. For your heart will always be where your riches are.' The same basic thought inspires the famous saying 'It is much harder for a rich person to enter the kingdom of God than for a camel to go through the eye of a needle' (Lk. 18:25). Indeed, the subject of wealth was one of Jesus' favourite themes: 'Sell all your belongings and give to the poor' (Lk. 12:33) was addressed to all who heard it. More specific was the advice to the rich man who had kept all the commandments 'There is still one more thing you need to do. Sell all you have and give the money to the poor, and you will have riches in heaven; then come and follow me.' (Lk. 18:22).[2]

Christians today are inclined to be embarrassed by the stress on future reward. We have been taught for so long that morality is about acting disinterestedly, without thought for oneself, that it has become a basic assumption. But there is a real difference between attending to the needs of others, in loving them, and not having any regard for ourselves. In teaching us to look for the reward of heaven, Jesus is not undermining the nature of morality. In the first place, our reward in heaven is our fulfilment in the true knowledge and love of God, a very different kind of reward than, say, expecting a large pay rise, or a lottery win. In the second place, we are taught to give up our own comfort and security on earth, in order to serve one another, to provide for the needs of others, not ourselves.[3]

If Christian ethics is to do justice to the teaching of Jesus, then, it must emphasise that ethics has to be understood in the light of our

---

[2] A similar theme runs through the New Testament in relation to marriage, though less pervasively. Marriage is good — but is better to be single — in the light of the coming Kingdom.

[3] For a more extended discussion of heavenly reward as a motive for moral living, see O'Donovan, *Resurrection and Moral Order*, pp. 248–53.

end. The goal of our lives is perfection in God's kingdom. So far, it appears that this theme has not influenced our consideration of ethics, which has been based on the themes of creation and covenant love. How do a kingdom ethic, a creation ethic, and a love ethic, belong together? Do they mean different things?

2.   Creation, Covenant and Kingdom

In looking at creation and covenant love as the foundations for Christian ethics, we have apparently ignored the fact that the aim of morality is to prepare us for life with God. It has seemed that looking only at the past and present has left the future out of account. However, this is to overlook the way in which we have considered creation and covenant. We have emphasised the point that creation has a goal, that God's purposes are built into the pattern of creation, and that these are there to be discerned. Creation looks forward to its fulfilment in the **Kingdom**. It is even clearer than this with covenant love, for love is centred on the love of God, and love too finds its fulfilment in the Kingdom. So, since creation and covenant both point forward to the kingdom of God, there can be no difference of substance between a morality based on creation, one based on love, and one based on the Kingdom, since each is truly understood in the light of the others.

But looking at ethics from a different viewpoint does give a distinctive perspective. From the viewpoint of creation we consider the great variety and complexity of morality. There are many different kinds of moral demand, many moral topics, detailed thought about huge ranges of choices and decisions. From the viewpoint of the Kingdom we think more about the simplicity and unity of the moral choice. There is an either–or quality about morality, which is related to the fact that in the end we have to choose for or against God in Jesus Christ. The judgement separates us to right and left. If specific actions are weighed, nevertheless it is finally each individual human being who is judged. So from the Kingdom perspective we focus on the formation and direction of a person's whole life, their character. The variety of ethics stemming from our nature as created beings leads us to formulate a range of rules and principles for moral guidance, to help us make specific decisions. One of the dangers of moral rules is that, up to a point, it may be possible for us to keep them, and in keeping them think that we have reached an adequate level of moral achievement. The viewpoint of the kingdom reminds us that we cannot attain perfection by our own efforts, and that we need to repent and accept the forgiveness of God.

One of our key themes has been the point that morality is both simple and complex. We often find it difficult to hold these together. Indeed, a simple confusion about this is a big contributory factor to moral cynicism. For instance, it is not easy to see what we should think about the moral status of the newly conceived human embryo. In thinking about how we should regard these things, we find there are many different arguments and considerations to bear in mind. When does an individual human person begin? Is the beginning of a person to be found in a process of development, or at a very specific stage? Various different moral conclusions can follow from the way we answer these questions, but to answer them we have to think hard about scientific, medical and theological matters. But this is not all, because we need to consider also whether there should be a connection between the biological sources of an embryo (the biological parents), and those who will bear and bring up a child. Should these invariably be the same people or not? Answering this question leads us into a range of further questions about the meaning of parenthood, about sex and procreation. Nor is this the end, for there are more issues, such as those concerning the social control of such medical possibilities, the duties owed to future generations, etc. etc. In thinking about such complexities (very briefly alluded to here), we can easily make two errors. One is to say that because this is so intractable a moral question, clearly there cannot be Yes–No moral answers. If there are no moral clarities here, does that imperil moral clarity everywhere? If, in other words, there are many important questions to which there are no right and wrong answers, what is to become of the difference between right and wrong? Right and wrong come to seem like arbitrary human inventions. The other mistake is apparently the opposite one, but it rests on the same misunderstanding. This is to argue that because there is (we know) a clear difference between right and wrong, so there must be a simple correct answer to all moral questions.

In looking at the meaning of casuistry, the way in which moral rules actually work, we have seen one answer to these misunderstandings. Moral rules, and their application, cannot be any more or less simple than the life to which they apply. The work of casuistry, of interpreting, refining and applying moral rules, helps us appreciate the distinction between right and wrong, good and evil on which the rules are based. The task of telling the truth can require some skill in some situations. But the rule of truth-telling is based on the nature of God's truthfulness. The created power of speech is intended for truth. The goal of our lives includes the aspect of truthfulness. In addition to this, though, the goal of our lives is that we should be truthful, loving, peaceful, and faithful. All these qualities are united together in the perfection which is God's intention for us. It is, finally, this perfection which is the basis for the opposition between right and wrong. Morality rests on the separation between what is acceptable in the presence of God, and what is offensive and cannot appear before God. But this distinction is only partly known by human beings, as the Kingdom, and God himself, are only partly known. Our specific moral actions and discriminations are related to the final separation in the presence of God.

This is to present morality as a thoroughly Christian business. There seems a lot of continuity between a Christian ethic based on creation, and a general moral sense common to many religions and peoples. But to make such a strong connection between Christian belief and the very nature of morality may seem to make Christian morality something quite different from everyday morality. If Christian morality is different, in its roots, is it still relevant outside the Christian church? And if it is so much a part of Christian faith, how is it that so much Christian moral teaching often seems so conventional?

3. Living Truthfully amid Earthly Illusions

In the light of the Kingdom our true characters are revealed. What does it mean to say that we must be perfect? Perhaps we think that perfection is about being flawless. If we think this, however, there is a danger of concentrating so much on little details that we miss the wider picture. Is perfection more about the overall direction and character of our lives, which give meaning and substance to the details? It may be helpful to see what this means by taking the area of truth. Being a truthful person means more than merely telling the truth on specific occasions, or even on every occasion. Being a truthful person also means seeing through the illusions and self-deceptions by which we so often hide reality from ourselves. This is one of the claims made by Stanley Hauerwas. [4]

Hauerwas has pointed out that looking at Christian ethics from the perspective of human virtues and character draws our attention to different concerns than those involved in discussions of particular moral dilemmas. He makes clear that thinking about the shape of our life as a whole is often more important than making the right decisions in every instance. Of course our decisions are important, and they make a difference to the sort of person we are. The area of truth is one of his key themes. So, for example, it is more to the point to think about what it means to be people who live by the truth, than whether it is justifiable in a hypothetical scenario to tell a lie.

Hauerwas attempts to expose what he sees as some of the illusions of his society (the USA), which he characterises as 'liberal'. Liberal society claims that every person has the right and the duty to determine what is true for them. This claim follows fairly straightforwardly from the basic premise of liberal society that everyone should be as free as possible. Since everyone has the right to their own truth, it follows that we must believe that there is no such thing as moral truth. Instead, we argue that there is scientific truth, but that moral and religious truth is unknowable, if it exists at all. For a liberal society, the only kind of truth is abstract and universal. In opposing this, Hauerwas argues that we cannot escape our own history and traditions. In particular, Christians must be ready to claim their particular story as truth. Christian knowledge of God is not abstract, but it is bound up with the story of Jesus Christ, his life and death. Because Christians live with, and are formed by, this specific story, they are bound to challenge liberal illusions.

---

[4] Especially in his earlier books, such as *Truthfulness and Tragedy*, *A Community of Character*, and *The Peaceable Kingdom*.

Hauerwas looks in a number of directions in which he claims to identify the typical illusions of a liberal society. These are all connected in some way with key features of liberal society, such as the secular public life, technology, and economic prosperity. Its illusions are important to it partly because it fears the truth. Illusions are more comfortable, and it is often easier not to admit the full reality of such things as mortality, suffering, tragedy, and the lack of hope for the future.

In *A Community of Character* there is a striking illustration of this point, taken from the book *Watership Down*. Although this book about rabbits is at first sight a children's story, and perhaps at a second glance a book celebrating the English countryside, it is also a political allegory. Various rabbit communities are portrayed in the book, and they represent certain types of political society. There is a traditional society, an authoritarian, a democratic, and a 'liberal' society.[5] The liberal society turns out to be a warren kept by a farmer who provides food for the rabbits, and then sets snares for them. One implication of this from the rabbit point of view is that any rabbit may be liable, at any time, simply to disappear. The rabbit-heroes of the book (Hazel and his friends) arrive at the warren during their travels, and they are puzzled and troubled by what they find. They realise that the word 'Where?' is quite taboo, so much so that it is not acknowledged. Rabbits in the liberal warren do not even appear to hear questions which begin: 'Where . . . ?' In other ways too the liberal rabbits are unable to be honest and truthful. For instance, trust between rabbits is impossible. Hazel and company, in joining the warren, improve everyone else's chances of not being snared. Of course this is not explained to Hazel — how could it be? The apparently generous hospitality actually rests on a total deception. There is therefore a close connection between inability to live with the truth, openly and honestly, and lack of trust, companionship and community. Avoidance of the truth and the practice of deception are very destructive of good relationships. Hauerwas also points out that the liberal warren does not tell the famous stories and myths about the origins of rabbits, their history and triumphs. A community is significantly formed by

---

[5] These labels are supplied by Hauerwas. In fact the 'liberal' warren has no name in the book, so we will call it 'the liberal warren'.

the stories it tells about itself, which give it a shared account of its history, convictions, purposes, and ideals.

Richard Adams' allegory of a secular liberal society chimes in very closely with Hauerwas's own diagnosis. There is perhaps one important difference. Where, in *Watership Down*, the main problem the rabbits have is the inability to come to terms with death, Hauerwas sees secular liberalism as having a number of illusions. It is impossible to do justice to the range and subtlety of his suggestions.[6] Here are some of the suggestions he makes, some in simplified form. A secular liberal society cherishes the following illusions:

1. Happiness is a sufficient goal for individuals, and society does not need any shared goals beyond that.
2. We can have a just society without individual people being just.
3. Society can overcome the lack of basic agreement and trust by increasing its abundance of possessions and technological power.
4. There is no such thing as moral tragedy, for 'there is always the right thing to do.'
5. A secular society has reason for hoping and trusting in the future.[7]

The last two need some further explanation. By moral tragedy Hauerwas means that there are occasions, and indeed continuing ways of life, where doing what is morally right does not have good consequences. If, for instance, the church is a community committed to nonviolence and truthfulness, then it may turn out to have a very unsettling effect. For telling the truth may disturb people in their comfortable illusions, and living without violence may threaten an order which is based on violence or the threat of violence. Hauerwas writes:

> 'For example, it is particularly important that such a community [the church] maintain the connection between truthfulness and nonviolence. For violence is often the result of the lies and half-truths we perpetrate on one another. And when the falsehood is discovered it becomes the seed of resentment and hate, inviting retaliation and violence that often takes the form of another lie. Therefore the church must be a community that demands truthfulness in all its dealings with one another and the world. Of course, it is often hard to know what the truth is and that too must be admitted truthfully'.[8]

---

[6] See, e.g. *The Peaceable Kingdom*, pp. 142–6 for a typical example, on 'tragedy and peaceableness'.
[7] *A Community of Character*, pp. 76, 73, 82; *The Peaceable Kingdom*, p. 22; *A Community of Character*, p. 166.
[8] *The Peaceable Kingdom*, p. 133.

In a secular society, a great deal hangs on keeping in control and in everything turning out well. By contrast, Christians know that they are weak and sinful people, and that things do not always work out well. The point is that they can live with that because they know that Jesus was weak and suffered. The story of Jesus tells us that God is able to forgive our failures and finally redeem us from evil.

Hauerwas makes his point about hope most sharply when he asks why it is that people want to have children. He notes that many of the reasons people give for having children do not really seem adequate. They say things like 'Children are fun' or 'They are an expression of a couple's love' or 'It is just the thing to do'. However, in an age when we are committed to individual autonomy and self-fulfilment, these reasons are barely adequate to explain why anyone should go to all the trouble and expense of raising children. Hauerwas' point is that people actually have children because children are a sign of our confidence in the future, because there is reason to hope. If secular people have such a hope, however, it has no basis in our spoken and shared convictions. Christians, on the other hand, do have good reasons to hope.[9]

Most of the illusions which Hauerwas attempts to expose are relatively subtle. He makes no claims that all modern liberal societies are the same in every detail, or that the church is any kind of ideal society, where society's mistakes are not also made. What is important is that the church should try to live as a community of trust, of hospitality, of peace, of truth, and of honesty about its own failures. Such a community may not be very successful, and it may not have all the answers. But it is still able to live joyfully while admitting its own weaknesses and failures. The fact that it does not have answers to questions raised by suffering and moral tragedy is alright, because Jesus himself lived and died with such questions.

Here we can return for a moment to the topic of euthanasia. Here Hauerwas might point out that it is our first concern to learn to live with the fact that we cannot always control pain, or the manner and time of death. This is more significant than knowing exactly what is the 'right thing to do' in treating a patient, knowing when to strive for life, and when to stop struggling. In fact, only when we can truly

---

[9] See *A Community of Character*, chs. 8–10.

live with the realities of pain, suffering and death, will we be able to approach making good decisions. Putting the decisions first, as our only priority, may blind us to the fact that we are not in control. We deceive ourselves about our success in coming to terms with death itself. Of course the actions taken in caring for the patient are important, and we have to attend with care to the detailed day by day decisions which may be necessary. We have already seen how those decisions are best taken within a Christian understanding of death, recognising the ambivalence of Christian faith about the fact that we are mortal. What Hauerwas would emphasise is the further truth that we can live without being in control of death, and without always knowing with certainty what is the right thing to do.

4.   Moral Knowledge in the Light of the Kingdom

We have seen a paradoxical element in Hauerwas's claims about the nature of moral goodness. He says both that we can begin to live as citizens of the Kingdom, in a truthful and peaceful way of life, and at the same time that we struggle to know what truth is, how to be peaceable, and so on. Our moral understanding is inevitably imperfect. Another writer who has made this point, but in quite a different way, is Oliver O'Donovan.

O'Donovan argues that all our knowledge of right and wrong is provisional, in the sense that all faith is provisional. It is only from the viewpoint of the Kingdom that we can see the simple unity of God's intention for us. Final discernment of good and evil, in general and in specific terms, can only be made in the light of the Kingdom. 'We can speak of the simple choice for or against God's new creation, the simple alternative of a broad way and a narrow way, the straightforward either-or opposition of sin and virtue.'[10] O'Donovan is at pains to make clear that the final simplicity of this choice does not allow us to say that all moral discernment is simple. We still find perplexity in trying to care in the best way for a dying person, discerning how to tell the truth in times of war, or how to respond to the huge variety

---

[10]   *Resurrection and Moral Order*, p. 260.

of legitimate claims on our available resources of money, time and energy.

Hauerwas and O'Donovan agree, then, on the irreducible complexity and obscurity of moral choice. Neither is prepared to go along with the claim that there is always one right thing to do, if only we knew what it was.[11] O'Donovan has a further claim to make, beyond the obscurity of moral knowledge, and the inevitability of moral conflict. The further claim is that the fundamental distinction between right and wrong, our knowledge of moral goodness, and the nature of Christian love are all only understood provisionally, in the light of faith. He argues that we cannot know the true nature of moral goodness any better than we know God. The true, full nature of love is only to be revealed to us when Christ himself is revealed in glory. 'The moral life of mankind is a moment in God's dealing with the created order which he has restored in Christ. Only as that restored order is fully disclosed can the meaning of human morality be comprehended . . . The true moral life of the Christian community is its love, and its love is unintelligible except as a participation in the life of the one who reveals himself to us as Love, except, that is, as the entry of mankind and of the restored creation upon its supernatural end'.[12]

This claim may sound shocking, especially if (as we are) we are committed to claiming confidence in morality. It is important, then to consider O'Donovan's claim carefully. His claim is that we do not know morality in the way we thought we did. It is a common assumption that we know the truth about certain things. We know our names and addresses, our job, our friends and family. We know gravity and other laws of nature, and so on. There is other more important truth that we think we know. We think we know the truth about ourselves, with a certain amount of self-examination; we know when we have done wrong and failed to live up to our own standards. Christians say 'I know God', and that they know that God is love. Knowledge of right and wrong is knowledge more like knowledge of self and of God, than knowledge of certain facts. If we think about it,

---

[11] The claim that there is always one 'right' decision is usually associated with the name of Kant.

[12] *Resurrection and Moral Order*, p. 246.

we realise that we are in part a mystery to ourselves. We more easily admit that God is a mystery. In the same way, complete knowledge of love is beyond us. Our knowledge of moral perfection is only as good as our knowledge of God. 'Be perfect, as your heavenly Father is perfect'.

The claim that our moral knowledge is imperfect is a totally different claim from the view that morality is subjective and relative. We have suggested qualifications to our moral certainty — that moral choice can be complex, that there is sometimes moral conflict, and that we do not yet know the fullness of moral goodness. None of these qualifications in any way undermines our basic confidence in the existence of moral truth, or in the claim that we have reasonable understanding of it. These qualifications also help us avoid certain kinds of legalism and moral self-righteousness. Our moral discernment is subject to the same kind of failure as any of our moral strivings. We stand in need of forgiveness for our lack of understanding, just as we need forgiveness for moral disobedience, selfishness, and pride.

Eleven

Forgiveness and Moral Rigour

Forgiveness is at the heart of the gospel, and yet it often seems to many that in practice it can compromise or even threaten high moral standards. As with all moral enquiry, to understand the issue clearly we need to begin with the gospel itself.

So far we have worked on the basis that the themes of covenant love and creation are a sufficient basis for Christian morality. We have assumed, in effect, that the theme of the kingdom of God is compressed into our understanding of covenant love. An essential feature of Christian morality is that the goal of our lives gives us moral direction, just as much as the starting place. We have emphasised the creation, the source or beginning of our lives; now we need to think also about the end, or goal, of human life.

At the heart of the Christian good news is the declaration from God that he wishes to bring us into his kingdom by his grace, not because of our merit. The meaning of salvation is that we are made children of God, treated as righteous, allowed into the presence of God despite our unworthiness. Our wrongdoings are forgiven, forgotten, put on one side as if they had not happened. By his gift of the Spirit, God transforms us into the likeness of his son Jesus Christ. The temptation of good people is so often to believe that they can correct their own character and behaviour, making themselves good enough, and worthy of reward for their moral goodness. It is easy for such people to suppose that without the promise of such reward, and the threat of losing it, people will not make the effort to be virtuous. But the gospel centrally and explicitly denies these two notions. The good news is that although we cannot be good by our own effort of will, that does not cut us off from God. Nor does the fact that we are rewarded, not for our goodness, but in spite of our wrongdoing, mean that we have no reason to amend our lives.

The idea of forgiveness has two essential implications for Christian morality. First, as we have already seen, the motivation for moral living is that of response to what God has done, and expectation of what he will do. It is not the motivation of fear of failure, or the need to reach a certain moral standard, that drives us to virtue. The second implication is clearly spelled out by Jesus: 'If you forgive others the wrongs they have done to you, your Father in heaven will also forgive you. But if you do not forgive others, then your Father will not forgive the wrongs you have done' (Matt. 6:14–15).

Because we are forgiven, we must also forgive others. We notice at once that God's free forgiveness claims us immediately. Being forgiven clearly does not mean that we are free to go off and behave just as we wish. But how can we freely forgive others and expect to maintain moral standards?

This question can take various forms, and it is similar to the question about the behaviour of the Christian who is forgiven. Let us list some of the key questions that arise.

1.   If Christians are freely forgiven, what is there to stop them from continuing to sin? Should they even sin more freely, so that the goodness of God's grace will be even more apparent? Should Christian really make a moral effort, and if so, why?

2.   If Christians are freely to forgive others, what basis does that give for a well-behaved and virtuous society? How will we hold people to moral standards? This is a real question for the administration of church discipline, just as much as for the administration of civil justice.

3.   In specific terms, can Christians play their part in upholding civil law, which expects people to be accountable for their actions? Can a Christian be a policeman or a lawyer, or will he simply have to pardon wrongdoers?

4.   Is it really feasible and sensible for our everyday lives to be conducted on this basis? Can the bullied wife, or the exploited office junior, simply go on forgiving and being exploited? Even if this were humanly possible, would it really be desirable, since it would simply allow the bully free rein? Should we not stand up for ourselves?

5. In other instances, it would seem that there simply is no practical chance to forgive. What would it mean for the grieving widow to forgive those who had killed her husband, if she will never know who they are, let alone meet them? Or if we are victims of crime, and the offender, once apprehended, shows no sign of remorse or repentance, what can forgiveness mean in such a case?

The variety of these questions should alert us to two general points. One concerns the fact that there is a limit to how much one can generalise about forgiving across the range of human experience, all the evil things which are done. The other point is that one aspect of forgiveness is the inner attitude of the forgiver. For all sorts of reasons, it may not be possible or appropriate for the inner attitude to control every action which is taken. It is sometimes really obscure whether a person has actually reached a secure place of forgiving, in their inner attitude. There is no way in which one can give a comprehensive account of human life. Each matter of forgiveness can only be rightly considered in its own right, in its own circumstances and setting.

People have done, and continue to do, terrible things to each other. People are murdered, tortured, raped. More domestically, people are abused physically, sexually and emotionally. We hurt each other in words and acts of deliberate and careless cruelty, and sometimes people endure years of injury from those they are close to. In response, all sorts of attitudes and actions may be appropriate. The abused person needs to be angry, to find healing and some form of restoration. Different people may go through a variety of processes and stages in order to come to terms with the way they have been treated. They may, perhaps need to confront their abuser in some way, or they may need to be protected and kept from them. In all sorts of ways, forgiveness may be more of a goal than a first step. If and when an attitude of forgiveness is arrived at in a positive and helpful way, then its expression may take all sorts of forms. It may have to remain an inner attitude, or it may need to be spoken.

It is the novelist rather than the moral theorist who can best explore the ways in which forgiveness works out. The novelist deals in stories, in relationships between people, and the connections between people's inner personalities and the things that happen to them. It is the novelist, too, who attempts to explore the inwardness of human life.

Since we do not know or understand ourselves all that well, and we only partly understand other people, there is plenty to explore. At times we may not really know if we have truly forgiven some wrong done to us, or whether we have only partly succeeded in covering up the hurt. We may conceal resentments and anger without recognising or dealing with them. Given that we are complex, and obscure even to ourselves, it is perhaps enough to hope that thinking about forgiveness will help us to recognise its importance for our lives and relationships. Since we may not even recognise whether or not we are forgiving, the gospel can help to alert us to the depths that are involved in this question.

With these cautions in mind, we can take our five questions one at a time. We must bear in mind that we can only make comments, since we cannot possibly give a comprehensive guide on 'How to forgive'. The first question, which asks about the difference between forgiveness and moral indifference, will set the pattern for all the rest, though clearly each question raises its own particular concerns.

Forgiveness and Moral Endeavour

Paul gave his answer to the first of our questions in his letter to the Romans, chapter 6. He has been at pains in the first five chapters to show that Christians are justified freely, that our righteousness is given to us by God and not earned by us. The action of the righteous man Jesus Christ has unilaterally cancelled the wrongdoing set in train by Adam. God's grace brings us to eternal life. In chapter 6, Paul raises as a rhetorical question the objection that had evidently been brought against his revolutionary teaching:

'Should we continue to live in sin so that God's grace will increase?' (verse 1), and 'Shall we sin, because we are not under law but under God's grace?' (v.15).

Twice Paul gives the same answer, in effect, beginning with the phrase translated as 'God forbid', 'Certainly not', 'By no means', 'Impossible!' The whole point of our forgiveness is that the power of wrong over us is broken, that we should live the new life of those destined for eternal life, not the old life, enslaved to wrong and heading for death. For Paul, we are either slaves of sin, or slaves of God, an insight which we can also express by saying that we cannot go in two different directions at once. We can only have one master, one purpose, not two opposed to each other. The point of turning round is to move in a different direction. The problem was that we could not turn of our own volition, for we were set in the old direction, slaves of sin. But the point of being united with Christ, accepted and forgiven, is to continue in the way of Christ. Why, Paul implies, should we have accepted forgiveness if we wished simply to remain in sin?

An important point follows from Paul's answer, which should be noted at once. His argument is all about the purpose of God's forgiveness, which is at one and the same time to deliver us from the power of wrong, and to bring us into relationship with him. Forgiveness of one another has two aspects. We should forgive others, both because we are forgiven by God, and so that we may not remain in enmity with those who wrong us, but if possible be in friendship. Obviously, since it takes two to make a relationship, that may not always be within our power. But at the outset forgiveness means renouncing feelings of animosity and the desire for revenge.

Forgiveness and Social Discipline

How then does forgiveness impinge on the maintenance of the social fabric, of the necessary moral standards, and the framework of law designed to uphold them? This is the second of our questions. In the first place, it simply does not impinge. As far as the maintenance of law is concerned, the business of educating children and disciplining offenders, this is just a different matter from the duty to forgive the one who wrongs us. The central aspect of the command to forgive is that it concerns our personal relationships. By this we include strangers and enemies, as well as those close to us. But the administration of justice is quite simply a different matter. This is not a particularly subtle point, nor one that removes anything from the duty to forgive. For instance, any parent knows the need both to forgive and to discipline their child. If they break something, it may be appropriate to insist that they pay for the damage, or contribute towards it, from pocket money. But this insistence has nothing necessarily to do with forgiveness. The unforgiving parent may still pay the bill, just as the forgiving one may ask for payment. Forgiveness has more to do with the restoration of love and friendship, than allocating the consequential costs. Practices of punishment and discipline have to do with maintaining and restoring the social fabric, so far as possible, when it is disrupted. Forgiveness does not mean simply ignoring offenses against the law and against other people, for forgiveness, like punishment, has as its ultimate aim putting things right.

But if forgiveness is irrelevant in the first place to the main structure of social discipline, it is not irrelevant to the manner of its administration. Two examples of the way **justice** and **punishment** are administered will be enough to make this clear. There are ways in which an offender can effectively be forgiven in sentencing, while not diminishing the reality of a crime. A judge has a number of possible options if convinced that an offender can effectively be forgiven. Suppose someone commits a crime under extreme pressure or provocation, for which they have clearly suffered and of which they equally clearly repent. Such a person can be convicted of the offence, and punished with a fine or prison sentence. Alternatively of course they could be put on probation, or given a suspended sentence, both options which combine an element of punishment with an element of forgiveness. Or in some cases the judge can decide on a discharge. Forgiveness is also relevant when we insist that someone who serves the sentence for a particular offence should then no longer be treated as an offender. There is an important practical point here. If someone who commits a crime is unable to get honest work ever again, then there may be little choice but to continue in crime. Society intends that a line should be drawn, and the past officially forgotten, in order for the criminal to be restored and the social fabric not to go on being threatened by his criminal activity. There is scope here for careful attention to individual cases, or types of crime and personality, but again the idea of forgiveness is important, and has a valuable practical role to play.

Forgiveness and Church Discipline

Forgiveness does have a part to play in the institutions of social **discipline**, in school, in the courts, and in church. For the most part, churches in Britain find it hard to maintain any substantial structures of discipline, but there is one area in which they remain relevant. The church can discipline people by excluding them, from such events as communion, baptism, marriage, absolution, and burial. Excommunication is but rarely practised nowadays, funerals are rarely if ever denied, and baptism is not often denied (though it is sometimes made difficult). But the Church of England (among other churches) finds marriage discipline a most trying problem in a society where divorce is common. Does forgiveness have an institutional role to play in considering whether someone may be remarried after divorce?

A covenant ethic of marriage accepts that the commitment of marriage can sadly come to an end. It is not the case that an indissoluble bond is created by a marriage ceremony, from which it is simply impossible to release people. Rather, a marriage is created by the mutual commitment of husband and wife, a commitment which is intended as a permanent commitment, as strongly as possible. If that marriage comes to an end, then that is a failure, but it is not actually an impossibility. At some point, before the death of either partner, the mutual commitment may in fact cease to exist any longer. At some stage, this separation is legally recognised as a divorce. If a divorced person then later wishes to remarry, the church has to consider the appropriate discipline. This discipline is appropriate (just as it also is before any marriage, or before baptism, for example). The church needs to ask whether it can permit someone who has failed to keep their marriage vows to repeat them to another person. There are a number of possible disciplines it can exercise, such as asking the couple to delay, or undertake some further preparation and counselling; refusing to marry a particular couple; or refusing to marry anyone. There are various questions it will need to ask concerning the earlier marriage and its legacy, about the new relationship and the readiness for another marriage. Is an old mistake simply being repeated? Are any children well cared for? Is there a willingness to learn and forgive? And so on. In all this the church must make provision for institutional discipline and forgiveness. As we have seen, forgiveness does not mean abandoning discipline. But it should play a significant role in these decisions, and in formulating a policy to handle them. There are both theological and practical reasons for this.

Some argue that the marriage vow is so solemn that it is in effect impossible for the church to forgive its breaking. In practice, remarriage after divorce is recognised in that the remarried are not excommunicated. It is not altogether easy to see the consistency of giving communion to those who are believed, in effect, to be living in a state of permanent adultery.[1] However, such people may be barred from remarriage in church, on those grounds, and also, until recently, from selection for ordination. The logic of all this is hard to recognise. There is more to be said for accepting the reality of remarriage, while insisting that the church should preserve its emphasis on the permanence of marriage by not conducting second weddings. This approach accepts that marriage breakdown is forgivable. Those who insist that remarriage can never be acceptable seem to allow no place for forgiveness. This is a serious theological oversight. It is also practically unhelpful. Structures of discipline, as we have noted, need to make a place for restoration of the wrongdoer. Even if it was true that the divorcee is necessarily a wrongdoer in remarrying, there is a place for restoration.

Can the Christian police officer forgive?

The recognition that society has a need to maintain institutions of discipline, and that this does not contradict forgiveness, quickly answers the question about Christians serving as police, lawyers and so on. Since it is right for society to punish wrongdoers, there is no objection to Christians playing their part in this work. As teacher, prison officer, probation officer, the Christian cannot simply forgive offenders. However, this is not to imply a sharp distinction between the Christian impulse to forgive, and the institutional role of having sometimes to punish. The Christian does not leave Christian faith behind when fulfilling a particular social role. Those who have the responsibility of disciplining others, maintaining institutions of discipline, will keep a special eye for possibilities of forgiveness, to see when that could accomplish the work of restoration more effectively than punishment. Obviously that depends on individual judgement and relationships in each instance.

---

[1] Andrew Cornes (in *Divorce and Remarriage*, p. 402) suggests that the remarried are to be thought of as polygamous. It is not clear to me how this squares with his case against remarriage after divorce, namely that it is adultery. A relationship cannot be both adulterous and polygamous at the same time!

Can we go on Forgiving for ever?

As private individuals, how often should we forgive, and go on forgiving? This was a question asked of Jesus by Simon Peter: 'Lord, if my brother keeps on sinning against me, how many times do I have to forgive him? Seven times?' 'No, not seven times,' answered Jesus, 'but seventy times seven, because the Kingdom of heaven is like this' (Matt. 18:21–23).

Jesus then went on to tell a parable, of a king who forgave a servant a large debt. But the servant then demanded a much smaller debt from another servant, whereupon the king sent for him and required the whole large debt. Christians owe it to others to forgive, because so much has already been forgiven them by God. Nor is there any end to this, because there is no end to God's forgiveness either.

Jesus' teaching here is characteristic of his style. There is the note of hyperbole — we must go on forgiving until we have counted into the hundreds — so in effect we do not even try to count occasions. But this apparent exaggeration rests on a very straightforward logic. This logic starts from God's perspective, the perspective of the Kingdom. To enter the Kingdom is only possible by the forgiveness and mercy of God. The debt we are forgiven by God is massive, a different order of magnitude from anything owed to us by any fellow human. Though we have right on our side, and we pursue a just cause in calling in the debts owed to us by others, still we are bound to forgive such debts because we have been forgiven so much. For if we wish to pursue justice, then we too will have to pay for our own moral offenses. What appeared to be hyperbole is only commonsense. It is, however, only commonsense from the perspective of Jesus, contrasted with the more down-to-earth viewpoints we usually adopt.

How can this be practical in everyday life? Should someone who is bullied simply go on putting up with it without protest? Is it not right to stand up for ourselves? If so, how can we do so and still go on forgiving? We should first note that the theological logic of Jesus' approach is immensely strong. Behind the evident, and typical, one-sidedness and exaggeration of his saying, stands the major truth of the gospel. This is a saying which we should take with literal seriousness. There is perhaps more common sense in this than we often admit. Everyday life is full of occasions when we offend each other in all sorts of ways, sometimes deliberately, but more often without any intention of doing so. Any close friendship or family life knows this well enough if it is to be both close and happy. Maybe we think we are making heroic efforts to forgive the other, while all the time they believe they are doing the same for us! There is good commonsense here for any two way relationship. But what of a more one-sided relationship?

There is also common sense here, for instance, for the junior colleague. It is better to be patient with an arbitrary and irascible boss. It does little good to continue grumbling and building up resentment. It is no more than common sense to be patient rather than irritable, to ignore or overlook snubs than to take them to heart, to carry out unnecessary chores without resentment. Perhaps such a reaction will soften the harshness, and bring about a better relationship. But to say only this is to open the way for Peter's question. Surely, he suggests, it cannot be right to go on and on forgiving for ever. There must come a limit sooner or later.

The impact of Jesus' saying is that there is no limit. Long after the time when it is clear that forgiveness has no practical effect in restoring relationships or softening the offender, we should go on forgiving. The reason for forgiveness has to do, not only with the desire to improve relationships, but fundamentally with God's forgiveness of us. We seem to be left with an impossibility. Apart from anything else, it seems morally undesirable to go on forgiving, and thus encouraging the wrongdoer to continue. Should the battered wife simply forgive her husband? Should the child sexually abused by her father say nothing? After we have taken the full measure of Jesus' words, surely this is not what he intended. To see why it is not so, we should note the point made a little earlier about the distinction between public and private roles.

Just as someone carrying out a public role is not simply a teacher, policeman, but also a Christian, an individual, so an individual also has a social, or public, role. Here is the point at which 'resistance' to wrongdoing should also play its part, along with forgiveness. The battered wife and the abused child have a responsibility to themselves and to others to see that such abuse is brought to an end. Wider society, after all, has an interest in healthy marriage customs; it certainly has an interest in seeing its children grow up properly cared for and respected. There is a point at which a proper self-concern is our responsibility to others also. This point may well come for the bullied office junior, for the whistle-blower who exposes corporate misdoing. Our concern for the social fabric, and for putting things to rights where we can, does not exclude forgiveness either. It is no doubt difficult for the policeman to forgive the armed robber, at the same time as pursuing and arresting him. But it is surely important for the policeman to be driven by a concern for justice, rather than by hatred or a desire for revenge. Forgiveness is an attitude of the spirit as well as specific action.

Forgiving Strangers

Our final question asked about the private individual forgiving an unknown stranger. Here, where there is no relationship to be restored, how is forgiveness possible? We must tread with caution here, for there are many such terrible wrongs perpetrated in our violent world, and we have no right to prescribe impossible demands which we cannot have faced ourselves. It seems to me that there are two things which can be said, as matters of principle, one negative and one positive. Negatively, it is personally most damaging for people to be eaten up with an unrequited desire for justice or revenge. While it is wrong to ask victims to think well of their oppressors, it is good that they should not actively hate them. Forgiveness at least requires the surrender of the desire for revenge, that the oppressor should suffer the same or more than was inflicted. Positively, all that can be said is that it is good to dwell on how much we have been forgiven. The love of God for us brings our forgiveness, but at the cost of Jesus' life given for us. Of this the Christian is reminded at every communion service 'This is my blood, shed for you and for many for the remission of sins'. We are brought back again to the central dynamic of the Christian good news.

The beauty of the virtue of forgiveness has been displayed by Gordon Wilson, the man whose daughter was killed by an IRA bomb in Northern Ireland. Wilson declared in public that he forgave his daughter's killers. These were not empty words, as shown by his later actions in meeting with Republican leaders, when he tried to persuade them to stop their campaign of violence. It was notable that his attitude of forgiveness was not a matter of being soft. When it became clear to him that the IRA had no intention of listening to his appeal and altering their policy, he was not committed to pious wishful thinking. That he forgave them had no substantial effect in creating any real relationship between him and them. He seemed to be the only one ready to open the possibility of such a relationship. The teaching that we should forgive has two aims in view, those of displaying something of God's love, and establishing a restored relationship. But even when creating relationship proves impossible, there is no need to think that forgiveness is pointless. In forgiving and being ready to forgive, we show ourselves to be true children of God.

In this chapter we have assumed that the problem we have is learning to forgive. We have assumed, that is, that we can start from the fact that we are forgiven by God, and that this is unproblematic. But, as Hauerwas reminds us,[2] we have first to learn what it means to be forgiven. If we can accept that we must receive forgiveness from God, which may be hard enough, we have also to be able to receive forgiveness from others. This can be harder, as it means admitting our sin, not denying it, and putting ourselves in the power of others. We have to be vulnerable to them. Hauerwas writes:

'It is true, of course, that in a sense to be a "forgiven people" makes us lose control. To be forgiven means that I must face the fact that my life actually lies in the hands of others. I must learn to trust them as I have learned to trust God.'

So far from forgiveness being an easy option, or threatening a sense of moral rigour, the moral demand to give and receive forgiveness is one of the mostly distinctively demanding things about Christian morality. It is a demand which Christians must consider central, and Christ gives the resources to live with such a demand.

---

[2] *The Peaceable Kingdom*, p. 89.

Twelve

The Bible and Christian Ethics

Chapter 12 may seem rather late to introduce the Bible in a book which aims to give a biblical account of Christian ethics. So far, however, we have been concerned to see how ethics belongs to the whole of Christian faith. Understanding morality is not so much about obeying particular commandments in the Bible, as seeing how morality works and makes sense in a Christian view of life. With that in mind, this chapter will merely take up a few general aspects in response to the general question: 'How can we best learn from the moral commands in the Bible, and the way it typically thinks about morality?'

Moral understanding follows from beliefs about the nature of God's love, his purposes for the created world, and his plan to redeem humanity from the power of evil. The primary use of the Bible for ethics is in teaching us these truths, the foundations for morality. In building the connections between doctrine and ethics, we can follow the Bible's lead as it gives moral commands and examples. But this is not quite the same as saying that we can simply take a biblical instruction and apply it today as moral teaching.

Some Dangers

The modern critique of the **literalist** approach to the Bible is too well known to need rehearsing here in detail. We are quite quick to see the point that we cannot simply understand Christian theology by quoting the Bible. To answer questions like 'Who was Jesus?' and 'Why did he die on the cross?' we need to think hard about the scriptures. The Bible is not sufficient on its own. Nor does it automatically answer questions about prayer, worship, mission and so on, though the Bible provides the main basis for areas like this. When it comes to ethics our reactions tend to be rather different. When Christians see a moral command in the pages of the Bible their first reaction tends to be that they must necessarily follow it literally. A moment's thought will show that accepting the Bible's authority does not imply literal obedience to all its moral teaching. We can avoid literalism without undermining the Bible's authority in moral matters. There is a clear distinction to be drawn between accepting the Bible's authority and taking all its commands literally.

We can outline three main reasons for avoiding literalism. It seems almost too obvious to say that biblical commands cannot simply be lifted off the page and taken as instruction for everyone today. Firstly, they must of course be read in their proper context. For instance, Jesus instructed one rich young man to sell all his possessions, give away his wealth and follow him. But this authoritative command, addressed to one person, did not apply to everyone Jesus met, and does not apply to everyone today in its literal sense. It does not claim everyone. But it still has authority in warning us all about the dangers of trusting in wealth, and facing us with the call to discipleship.

Secondly, the Bible was written in particular times and places. In the intervening centuries, many features of society have changed. It is not easy to analyse these changes accurately. We are people of our own time and culture just as much as biblical writers were of theirs. For instance, in a passage in 1 Corinthians 11 which is extremely obscure to us nowadays, Paul instructs that women must not attend public worship without covering their heads. It is easy to understand that social customs have changed in such a way as to make Paul's instructions inapplicable today. What is less obvious is that relationships between men and women, both in marriage and in society generally, were conducted in quite different ways in the Jewish and Greek cultures of the first century. Even less obvious is the fact that we are blind to the drawbacks inherent in our own ideals, the ideals by which we so often judge other cultures so harshly. Indeed, contemporary confusion about gender roles, about sexuality and sexual expression and about marriage itself, makes it if anything harder for us to see clearly in this area. But it also means that New Testament instructions about roles within marriage, about divorce and related matters, have to be treated with care before we adopt them without question. It is the underlying principles and understandings that we must seek to identify as best we can. This may or may not mean adopting biblical moral teachings as they were written.

Thirdly, the Bible tells us of God's unfolding plan of salvation. It tells of creation, of human rebellion, and of God's first calling of his people through Abraham and the patriarchs. It tells of the giving of the law and of the expectation of an anointed Messiah, a saviour. It tells of the coming of Christ, of his preaching about the Kingdom of God, of his death and resurrection. It tells of the ascension of Christ, the giving of the Spirit and the early growth of the Christian churches. Throughout this history, God instructed his people in particular ways. His instructions cover not only moral matters, but also particular events, religious and civil legislation. So, as we move through both Old and New Testaments, we have to have an eye for their context in the history of salvation.

For instance, the traditions of Sabbath and Sunday observance need to be examined from this angle. Stemming from its place in the ten commandments, the Sabbath command received detailed interpretation in Jewish religious teaching. But the New Testament puts a big question against the observance of the Sabbath. Jesus pointed out that its observance had become a burden rather than a freedom. St Paul resisted the necessity for Christians to observe particular days and festivals. Perhaps most striking of all, the writer of Hebrews argues that fulfilment of the Sabbath rest will be found in heaven. It also needs to be noted that the early Christians shifted the keeping of the Sabbath from Saturday to Sunday, in honour of the resurrection. Does this mean that the Sabbath law should no longer apply to Christians? Before moving to this conclusion, we should look at the original rationale given for the Sabbath. It is for rest and worship, because (and here the two lists of the commandments differ) God rested on the seventh day, and/or because he redeemed them from slavery in Egypt. In interpreting the relevance of the Sabbath in contemporary society, we need to bear these fundamental arguments in mind, as well as the great changes from ancient Israelite society to our own time.

These cautions about interpreting biblical commands with care do not diminish the Bible's authority. Indeed, its authority can only be properly followed when it is rightly understood. These cautions are also important because it is all too common for people to take biblical morality too literally in everyday devotional reading and study. This is perhaps particularly true of matters involving marriage in the New Testament. Christians argue at length about the legislative import of Jesus' sayings about divorce. Before we base church law on his saying that remarriage after divorce is adultery, we need to ask careful questions. In particular, what evidence is there that Jesus intended this teaching to be the basis for legislation? It seems much more likely that Jesus wanted to underline the solemnity of marriage vows, using the graphic exaggerations which typify his speech. It also needs to be asked what the practice of divorce was, against which his words were directed. It may be impossible to be totally sure of this, but the evidence suggests that divorce was an easy practice, in which women were cast aside and discarded in a casual way that was nevertheless legally acceptable. Now there are divorces like that in modern society, but it needs to be recognised that divorce is a much more varied phenomenon. In many cases today, divorce protects vulnerable women from cruelty and exploitation on their husband's part. We need to be very cautious before simply assuming that such divorces were the target of Jesus' vivid language.

Perhaps fewer Christians are inclined to take literally St Paul's injunction to wives to be submissive to their husbands. But this injunction causes heartache for husbands who feel they ought to be more 'in control' of their wives, in ways that seem not only out of step with modern society, but also other themes of New Testament ethics. It helps to recognise that the old prayer book promise made by brides to 'obey' their husbands is a mistranslation. The word consistently used in the New Testament for a wife's attitude to her husband means 'be subject to'. It is the word used for the proper attitude of all Christians to each other. It is not the word 'obey'. Obedience is the duty owed by slaves to their masters and by children to their parents. Having said this, there is an asymmetry in the relationship between husbands and wives as envisaged by St Paul. He charges wives to 'be subject' to their husbands, and husbands to love their wives. We are right to think this odd, not because our modern customs are different, but because of the clear pressure towards equality to be found in St Paul's writings.[1]

To understand this, we must not overlook the marriage customs of the first century world. It seems more than likely that Christian faith may have encouraged believers to rebel against the rigid, perhaps authoritarian, patterns of the time. If so, they may have caused trouble by their unruly or revolutionary behaviour. Against this background, St Paul can be understood as urging a relationship of love, but also of social decorum. Wives would commend the Christian faith, not by rashly claiming a new freedom, but by accepting their social status as a secondary matter, when set beside their salvation in Christ. In changed social times, therefore, Christians should be happy to find appropriate ways of expressing the key virtues of marriage in new social customs. Love and faithfulness are the moral priorities; it matters much less whether the marriage is formal or informal, whether the roles of husband and wife are rigid or flexible.

The Roots of Morality

So far, we have been concerned to avoid dangers in reading the Bible. It is more constructive to examine the way in which the Bible positively locates its own moral teaching. We have alluded to the varieties of moral instruction contained in the Bible. There are general commands and directives, such as the ten commandments; there is civil legislation, often with clear moral assumptions and implications; there is consideration of specific topics such as marriage or worry, money or hatred; there are exhortations to purity and a way of life; and much more. Some is practical, some idealistic; some addressed to specific actions or decisions, some to attitudes and emotions; some addressed to particular people and some apparently universal in its scope. There are some clear themes which remain central throughout, but there is a great deal of variety.

---

[1] And elsewhere in the New Testament.

One feature is particularly striking. From beginning to end ethical precepts and teaching are based on beliefs about what God has already done. The ten commandments are prefaced by: 'I am the Lord your God who brought you out of Egypt, where you were slaves' (Exod. 20:2). Amos, one of the most fiercely moral prophets, declares God's word to Israel: 'Of all the nations on earth, you are the only one I have known and cared for. That is what makes your sins so terrible, and that is why I must punish you for them' (Amos 3:2). We might expect to find an exception in the book of practical moral wisdom, Proverbs, but here also it is emphasised that: 'The fear of the Lord is the beginning of wisdom' (1:7, etc.). The same is even more true of the New Testament. Jesus taught: 'You must be perfect, just as your Father in heaven is perfect' (Matt. 5:48). 'If you forgive others the wrongs they have done to you, your Father in heaven will also forgive you. But if you do not forgive others, then your Father will not forgive the wrongs you have done' (Matt. 6:14–15). 'If you love me, you will obey my commandments' (Jn. 14:15).

For St Paul, the gospel means that we are made righteous, justified, through faith, freed and forgiven from our sins. Now we are free, not to continue in sin, but to live for righteousness. St John argues, like St Paul: 'This is how we know what love is: Christ gave his life for us. We too, then, ought to give our lives for our brothers' (1 John 3:16). He uses a variety of appeals to connect our relationship with Christ to the moral quality of our lives. For instance: 'But we know that when Christ appears, we shall be like him, because we shall see him as he really is. Everyone who has this hope in Christ keeps himself pure, just as Christ is pure' (1 Jn. 3:2–3).

Throughout the Bible we see that the same fundamental appeal is made. Because God is like this, because this is what he has done, because this is his love for us, because this is his plan for us, so you should live in corresponding ways. God has saved you, so obey him. God is love, so live in love. God is pure, so be pure. God will transform you by his grace, so you should act in accordance with that transformation. The nature of God, and the relationship he has initiated with us, provide the pattern and the motive for our morality. It is worth underlining that this rationale for Christian life supplies the complete basis for morality. There is no 'right and wrong' apart from the right and wrong inherent in living as the people of God. Indeed, the Christian claim is that the universal human sense of the difference between right and wrong itself stems from the way we are made. Knowing right from wrong is something that is learned as we grow up, and as we learn how to belong to our particular society. But the very sharp sense of moral claim on us stems, Christians believe, from the way God has put that within us.

The Bible also provides a variety of moral appeals, though they are nearly all rooted in appeal to the nature of Christian belief. There are commands, there are ideals, there are practical warnings and advice, general and specific appeals, and so on. There is in all this little if any appeal to **utilitarian** arguments, or anything that could be construed as supporting that kind of moral argument.[2] There is rather a heavy emphasis on the intrinsic quality of our actions, thought, speech, way of life. We are judged by the nature of what we do and who we are, not by the results of our actions. Appeals to the future (teleological arguments, as they are called) are directed to our actions as revealing the essential character of the actor, the direction in which we are headed. God wants to make us like Christ, so we should behave in a Christlike way. God wants to make us pure, so we should conduct ourselves with purity.

There is a clarity and sharpness about God's claim on our lives. This is a serious problem with utilitarian accounts of ethics, that they cannot give a good account of this quality of the moral claim. Here is another important contrast with an ethic based on values. As we have argued, the nature of values is that we choose them, and we weigh them, whether as individuals or as societies. So it is difficult if not impossible for such values to make any real claim on us, certainly with any strong imperative sense of claim.

Covenant ethics is an attempt to provide a coherent understanding of morality which articulates the essential characteristics of biblical

---

[2] Utilitarian arguments are those which see moral goodness as based on what brings the most happiness. More generally, utilitarianism is a type of consequentialism, i.e. any theory which bases what is right on the consequences of our actions. If something results in the best state of affairs, then it is the right thing to do. Such ways of thinking about ethics provide the basic assumptions for most moral arguments in our day.

morality. As we have seen, it finds in Christian love the central focus of biblical appeals to the nature of God. It is the claim of love on us that leads to the definite moral prohibitions of biblical ethics, and love which shapes the positive claim that the people of God should live in certain ways. The love of God for every individual lies at the root of the Christian concern for every individual human being. At the same time love sets boundaries to individualism, since we are all set in communities with duties of love to one another.

Love on its own does not give us enough guidance as to the detailed conduct of our lives in every area. The Bible offers many detailed precepts in many areas. These, we have argued, must be treated as authoritative, but not necessarily in their literal sense. To begin to show how we can make unified sense out of the variety of biblical material, it will be preferable to take a particular area for discussion. The human use of property provides an excellent example.

Property in the Bible

Jesus appears to have spent a lot of time teaching his disciples about the right attitude to money. He emphasised very strongly the dangers of wealth. It can keep us out of the Kingdom, it becomes a preoccupation, keeping us from attending to our service of God, and it is of little lasting worth. The disciple's priority is to follow the master, and to pay little attention to the things of this world which can hinder this. Riches are most dangerous because it is so hard to lay them aside. Contrary to appearances, it is not the rich who are blessed, for it is the poor whom God will call into his Kingdom.

There are only a few hints in the Gospels that Jesus was at all concerned with the enjoyment of God's world, or the necessity of money in everyday life. His speech clearly shows an appreciation of the natural world (for instance the famous passage about the lilies of the field, and the frequent images of sheep and shepherds). From time to time also, he showed awareness of the need and propriety of paying taxes, though relying on his Father to provide for this and for all daily needs from day to day. In this as in other areas of teaching, everything is subjected to the overriding concern with the Kingdom. To find a fuller picture, within which, at the centre, to put the teaching of Jesus himself, we can start with the book of Genesis.

The story of creation tells that all the goodness of the earth is provided for human beings. Humanity is put in charge of the earth. This view is expressed in both chapters 1 and 2. The story of the fall does not alter this in essentials, but now the earth will only give up its goodness unwillingly. 'You will have to work hard and sweat to make the soil produce anything'. In the spreading effects of the fall that follow in Genesis 4–11, greed is not a major theme. Hatred, ambition and revenge seem to be the main problems, though the picture is not spelt out in detail. Indeed, in the stories of the patriarchs, the possession of wealth is typically regarded as a sign of God's blessing. It is good to prosper, with many flocks, like Abraham, Jacob and Joseph. This is a continuing theme throughout the Old Testament, as we shall see. The story of human sinfulness is portrayed as continuing quarrelsomeness, jealousy, ambition, deceit and so on.

Laws concerning property, in Exodus and the Books of the Law, emphasise the part played by property in human disputes and rivalry. Of the ten commandments, two are relevant: 'Thou shalt not steal' and 'Thou shalt not covet your neighbour's house . . .' Desire for other people's property leads to injustice, disputes and so on. The more detailed laws of the Pentateuch are also concerned to protect private property. They also provide regulations as to how to handle various kinds of disputes over property — what to do if an animal strays, if it is injured while someone is borrowing it, how to resolve disputes, and so forth.

We should note at least four other important themes in Israel's laws. The goodness of the land is promised to the people as long as they continue to worship and obey the Lord. Prosperity is promised as a blessing from God. One of the ways in which obedience is expected is the dedication of offerings to God. Detailed regulations prescribe how the first fruits are to be set aside and offered in worship. There are commands which make provision for the needy, for strangers. Fields and vineyards are not to be harvested so methodically that there is nothing left to be gleaned: 'Do not go back through your vineyard to gather the grapes that were missed or to pick up the grapes that have fallen; leave them for poor people and foreigners' (Lev. 18:10).

Finally, land cannot be sold in perpetuity; it remains the property of the owner or his family, even if it is sold for a number of years. 'Your land must not be sold on a permanent basis, because you do not own it; it belongs to God, and you are like foreigners who are allowed to make use of it' (Lev. 25:23). There is doubt as to whether this law was ever fully and consistently applied, but it is important to note its intention and rationale.

In all this the desire for prosperity is not seen as problematic, provided that it is not obtained greedily at the expense of others, by ignoring the poor. Religious duties must not be neglected, and God's goodness recognised as the source of all prosperity. For the most part, the same themes are expressed in different proportions in the rest of the Old Testament. The book of Proverbs is full of promises that the righteous will prosper, and assumes that prosperity is a blessing from God. Prosperity is to be obtained by hard work; the idle will come to no good. However, honesty and wisdom are better than wealth, and it is certainly not good to get rich through injustice. Concern for the poor is occasionally voiced in Proverbs, but it is much more a theme of the prophets. Many of the prophets are full of condemnation for those who have gained wealth by injustice (taking bribes, using false measures, exploiting the poor). The religious sacrifices of the evildoer will not be acceptable to God. The prophets underline the fact that caring for the widow, and for the poor, are duties, not optional extras.

In general, then, we can summarise an Old Testament attitude to money and property along the following lines. There is a strong emphasis on the goodness of God's gifts, and the clear recognition that they come from him and should be received with thanks. There are definite temptations in wealth, especially that we will try to get rich by unjust methods, that we will use our wealth too selfishly, with insufficient regard for others, the poor and the stranger. There is also the danger of depending on our wealth, rather than trusting in God who alone is the true giver. What we have, especially the land, is given to us in trust; there are limits to our acquisition or disposal of our family's inheritance. If we lend to the poor, we are not to charge interest, and there are regulations which govern the taking of securities for loans. The laws given to Israel point to the kind of duties people owe one another, as well as erecting certain prohibitions and positive duties.

It is in the Psalms and in the book of Job that we find questioning as to whether the righteous will necessarily become rich. Here we find the recognition that evil men do often prosper, that the righteous may not always do well, and that wealth may be a distraction from trust in God. 'If riches increase, set not your heart on them' (Ps. 62:10); 'I delight in following your commands more than in having great wealth' (Ps. 119:14). Proverbs also recognised that 'When a wicked man dies, his hope dies with him. Confidence placed in riches comes to nothing' (Prov. 11:7).

But for all the awareness that prosperity must not be the centre of our lives, there is little in the Old Testament to prepare us for the radical challenge of Jesus. The Old Testament seems merely prosaic when set beside his sharp warnings. Is it possible to reconcile the day-to-day pragmatism of Proverbs, for instance, with the other-worldly approach of the Sermon on the Mount? Various different ways have been suggested of understanding the strenuous commands of Jesus, in order to relate them to them practical necessities of everyday life. First it will be helpful to see how the rest of the New Testament handles the question of property. What did the early church make of Jesus' warnings about wealth?

In the early days, from the day of Pentecost, with the heady excitement of the coming of the Spirit and the rapid growth of the church, there was a renunciation of private property. The first believers came together in close fellowship, sharing their belongings together. 'They would sell their property and possessions, and distribute the money among all, according to what each one needed' (Acts 2:45). The book of Acts makes clear that this practice continued. It is a central theme of the book for the first six chapters. But when the story turns to the conversion of Paul, beginning with the martyrdom of Stephen, the theme of sharing of possessions fades into the background. The missionary impetus required Paul to earn his own living, which he did by making tents (Acts 18:3).

Paul expected believers to share their money, (though he did not call believers to sell everything, or to share all their goods together). First, they should help the Christians in poorer churches, and this should be done in a planned and careful way, setting money aside each week (1 Cor. 16:2), so that those who had plenty shared with those who had less (2 Cor. 8:13). Another time, the sharing might be the other way round. Paul also believed that the churches should pay for the ministers who preached the gospel and taught the faith. These kinds of financial concern are considerably less far-reaching than the complete sharing described in the early chapters of Acts. There is certainly no sign in Paul's letters that he expected Christians to give everything away. Rather, he teaches them to work honestly to earn their living, to provide for their own needs and for the needs of others. The famous saying 'The love of money is the root of all evil'[3] is certainly a Pauline theme, but it is not particularly prominent in his ethical advice. The other NT letters also give advice on this. The fiercest critic of the wealthy is James: 'And now, you rich people, listen to me! Weep and wail over the miseries that are coming upon you! Your riches have rotted away, and your clothes have been eaten by moths' (Jas. 5:1–2). James' diatribe is directed against those who have made themselves rich by oppressing their workers, and against those who place their security in their wealth.

It is clear, then, that the early church did not find it appropriate to continue to share all possessions. Instead, the basic impetus is preserved in the insistence that we should not set our hearts on wealth, and that we should share from our plenty rather than seek to accumulate it and spend it on our pleasures. Though this catches the heart of Jesus' insistent teaching, it does not emphasise the point with the same strength and feeling. How can we best do justice to what Jesus actually taught?

We can set on one side the view that the church has sometimes held, that these teachings are only directed at the first class Christian, while the rest get along in a more everyday fashion. This view held that those who felt called to live in poverty were somehow better than those who did not. This is an unsatisfactory approach. Another possibility is to argue that Jesus habitually exaggerated to make his point. There are certainly many examples of this, such

---

[3] The sense is better given by 'The love of money is a root of all kinds of evil' (so NRSV, 1 Tim 6:10).

as: 'If your right eye cause you to sin, take it out and throw it away!' (Matt. 5:29) or 'It is easier for a camel to pass through the eye of a needle than for a rich man to enter the kingdom of heaven' (Lk. 18:25). This observation is certainly helpful, but it does not really explain why Jesus taught like this. For that, we must look at the reasons Jesus gave for making such one-sided demands of his followers. His concern was that we should be like our Father, perfect. Nothing less would do. In the light of our destiny, to be children of God, to inherit God's kingdom, to see God and receive his mercy and blessing, nothing on earth finally matters. Even our family ties and responsibilities, our own goods or our own lives, our property, our time, our health, none of these is of lasting significance when set beside the joys of obtaining God's reward. It is surely for this reason that Jesus so often exaggerated, to drive home his perspective, so that we could see it in all its starkness. So also Jesus characteristically abstracts us from all the ties and complications of social life. In the end, we must stand as we are before God. The many needs that claim us — to restrain evildoers, to provide for our family and ourselves, to work for a living — all these are insignificant beside the supreme urgency of preparing for the Kingdom.

In the light of this, we can see that the more routine transcription of Jesus' teaching about property and riches offered by Paul is not to be called a compromise. The essential point is that the Christian must sit loose to earthly goods, not to deny their goodness, but because more important things are at stake. Nor is this simply a matter of 'attitude', as some Christian teachers sometimes suggest. Our attitude is to be demonstrated in real giving, in providing for the needs of the poor, and for the work of the church.

The themes of the Old Testament must be understood from this viewpoint. It is not only in the treatment of prosperity that Jesus dramatically highlights one strand at the expense of others. As far as wealth is concerned, he makes clear that this is not to be seen as the main sign of God's blessing. God's goodness is much more solid than the transitory and unreliable benefits of riches. Indeed, riches are dangerous because they blind us to the better things. Jesus emphasised the strands of Old Testament thought which made this point.

We can suggest two other areas where there is a similar change of emphasis, or even of direction. The Old Testament saw childlessness as a curse. Jesus, on the other hand, taught the benefits of celibacy, of freedom to serve the Kingdom, to proclaim the good news. For him family life must not stand in the way of discipleship. The believer must be ready to leave all (even husband or wife) if the service of God calls for that. In the rest of the New Testament, we find more measured views about the duties of family members to each other. The value of celibacy is compared favourably with married life, but there is no insistence that it is always best for Christians to be single.

Another such case is that of war. There is a clear strand in the Old Testament which sees war as a necessity in the interests of the people of God. Jesus turned his back on militarism, insisting instead that there is no right for the Christian to defend himself, even against arbitrary military oppression. On the whole, the rest of the New Testament offers a more positive view of the need for human authorities, and the importance of their duties. The New Testament, however, comes to no clear resolution of this issue, setting up a divergence which has persisted among Christians almost ever since. Some are convinced that Christians should be pacifist, while others are convinced that the call of love and justice in an evil world may sometimes lead the Christian to take up arms.

Each of these three areas (property, marriage, warfare) gives examples of how important it is to understand biblical moral examples and precepts in their theological setting. Jesus did not teach the same as the book of Proverbs about the blessings of wealth, though there are elements in common as well as divergences. To grasp biblical morality as a coherent whole, we need a theological framework. In earlier chapters we have set out such a framework based on the fundamentals of Christian love and the doctrine of creation, and looking forward to the kingdom of God. Such a framework needs to be informed and corrected by detailed attention to biblical texts, while those texts themselves are understood within the overall framework. There is no short cut, nor is there completeness in this task. We can be confident that we will not be forced to revise the doctrine of marriage in significant respects. But the possibility remains even here that we may have to find new understanding to tackle new issues.[4] If we have strong biblically based theological foundations, we will be as equipped as we can be to tackle fresh questions.

---

[4] Oliver O'Donovan is fond of pointing to the newness of the fact that a child can now have three biological parents, not just the two that were possible up to 1980. This forces us to think carefully about the meaning of marriage and parenthood in new ways.

Thirteen

The Authority of Conscience?

An important feature of covenant morality is that moral truth is objective. This means that moral choice is at least as much a matter of discerning the truth as of making decisions. Moral truth does not depend on the subjective decision of the actor, on will or emotion. Nor does it depend on the consequences of the action alone, though these may help us to see what kind of action was actually performed. Whatever the place of **conscience** in the task of deciding what is to be done, it is not the conscience which can actually make an action right or wrong. The conscience, as we shall see, certainly has a place, but it must be properly instructed. Modern individualism, however, exploits certain strands in the Christian traditional understanding of conscience to make it arbiter in a world of individually chosen moral values. It is important that covenant ethics distinguishes its understanding of conscience from the characteristic modern view.

The conscience has a proper authority in making moral decisions. But that authority has become greatly exaggerated, and in secular ethics it exercises great sway. In order to examine the various uses of the word 'conscience', and to see how we have arrived where we are, it is perhaps easiest to trace the development of the idea of conscience. To begin with, this happened within Christian theology.

Conscience in the New Testament

The word conscience makes an important appearance in the New Testament, but it is not given a major place. The classic study of the subject remains C.A. Pierce's *Conscience in the New Testament*, published in 1955 but not nearly as well known or influential as it should be. Pierce's main points can be easily summarised. It was Paul who used the word; apart from Paul it occurs only in Hebrews and 1 Peter. The background for Paul's usage is its use in everyday Greek, though Paul was probably prompted by the use made of the word by some of his opponents in Corinth. Pierce traces a number of shades of meaning, but the basic idea is this: conscience is the pain felt by someone after they have done something which they know to be wrong. It is always used with reference to a past event, and mostly after wrong doing. Occasionally someone may say that they have a good conscience, in other words that they are not suffering the pain of conscience. Pierce summarises his study: 'Conscience in the New Testament is the painful reaction of man's nature, as morally responsible, against infringements of its created limits . . .'

Conscience can be in error for a variety of reasons, such as misunderstanding moral requirements, or through false information, or through force of habit (perhaps when the pain of conscience is repeatedly ignored, and the pain is dulled). Pierce continues: 'St Paul would have granted that, for all its liability to error, conscience must be obeyed . . . He is definite that conscience only comes into play after at least the initiation of a wrong act; when it does not come into play [. . .] it can never mean that the action was more than "not wrong" — that it was "right" in the sense, even, of the only or best possible in the circumstances; still less can conscience have anything to say directly about future acts.' (pp. 108–109).

Pierce goes on to draw a vigorous contrast between this use of conscience and characteristic modern Christian teaching. One definition is that 'The orthodox view is that wherever two courses of action are possible, conscience tells me which is right, and to choose the other is sin.'[1] Pierce again summarises: 'Conscience, then, is taken today as justifying, in advance or in general principle, actions or attitudes of others as well as one's self. But in the New Testament it cannot justify; it refers only to the past and particular; and to the acts of a man's own self alone' (p. 117).

---

[1] Russell, quoted by Pierce, p. 114.

Different Meanings of Conscience

Clearly the word 'conscience' turns out on examination to have more than one characteristic meaning. A good deal of the difficulty experienced in Christian teaching about conscience stems from confusing these different meanings. We can follow the lead given by Pierce in setting them out. First, there is the perception that our conscience pricks us when we have done something wrong, or are about to. Our conscience brings to our mind that it is wrong to steal, if we see an unattended pile of coal that we could make use of ourselves. The coal does not belong to us, but to someone else. Taking it would be theft, and there is no question that theft is morally forbidden. Even if we had 'no conscience' about taking the coal, there would be no question that what we did was wrong. Conscience simply prompts us to do what is right; it does not decide what is right. This is an extension of the New Testament sense. We know that if we did take the coal, we would suffer the pain of conscience. The first meaning, then, concerns the application of known moral principles to particular actions. It applies primarily to wrong actions actually done, and by extension to wrong actions contemplated.

The second characteristic meaning of conscience is that it is the judge of what would be the right thing to do. We 'consult' our conscience to help us decide on a particular course of action. It is important to notice that this may be done in a number of ways. For instance, someone may say they are following their conscience when they follow a complex framework of thought and apply it to a variety of different choices. A doctor or social worker may do this in making awkward decisions about priorities and so on. Such decisions are a complex mixture of reason, intuition and judgement. In quite a different way, someone else may claim to be following their conscience when they take some action that seems congenial and right at the time. It may be that they feel happy, or that they have seriously considered relevant moral principles. Or it may be that their feelings are simply being given sway over and above any moral concern.

The contrast between these two very different uses of the concept of conscience are well expressed by the Pope, in an extract from *Veritatis Splendor* which is worth quoting at length:

> Certain currents of modern thought have gone so far as to *exalt freedom to such an extent that it becomes an absolute, which would then be the source of values* . . . The individual conscience is accorded the status of a supreme tribunal of moral judgment which hands down categorical and infallible decisions about good and evil. To the affirmation that one has a duty to follow one's conscience is unduly added the affirmation that one's moral judgment is true merely by the fact that it has its origin in the conscience. But in this way the inescapable claims of truth disappear, yielding their place to a criterion of sincerity, authenticity and "being at peace with oneself" . . .
>
> 'Conscience is no longer considered in its primordial reality as an act of a person's intelligence, the function of which is to apply the universal knowledge of the good in a specific situation and thus to express a judgment about the right conduct to be chosen here and now. Instead, there is a tendency to grant to the individual conscience the prerogative of independently determining the criteria of good and evil and then acting accordingly. Such an outlook is quite congenial to an individualist ethic, wherein each individual is faced with his own truth, different from the truth of others.'[2]

Thomas Aquinas and conscience

To see how the Christian view of conscience has developed since its early use in the New Testament, we need to look at Thomas Aquinas. First, we must briefly explain Thomas Aquinas' doctrine of **natural law.** Aquinas expressed it like this. All law stems from God. God's eternal law determines the nature of things. It is simply expressed by the natural world – the stars and planets, the laws of gravity, of life and growth. God's eternal law also describes how human beings should behave, but humans are given the task of reasoning that pattern out for themselves. In discovering this, human beings have a rational apprehension of the eternal law. Each person knows fundamentally, for instance, that lying, cheating, stealing and killing are not good, and that loving, truth-telling, and justice are better. To this extent, human beings 'participate in' God's eternal law. It is this rational participation that Aquinas calls natural law. In support of this we can readily admit

---

[2]   *Veritatis Splendor*, para. 32, pp. 52–53. Italics in original.

that all human societies distinguish between right and wrong, and that there is a good deal of common ground in what is considered right and what wrong, in widely separated human cultures.[3] The content of this basic general moral apprehension is called natural law. Natural law needs to be amplified and corrected by God's revelation ('positive divine law'). The label conscience is then given to the human faculty by which we receive natural law. Our conscience teaches us 'that it is wrong to steal, to deceive, and to commit other sins'. In this idea of conscience, it is the conscience itself which perceives the content of morality. It is not simply that our conscience applies what is already known, but it both decides and applies the content of morality.

This led Aquinas to a classic problem. Is it right to act against the dictates of a mistaken conscience? There is no really satisfactory answer to this question. Suppose we were to say that one should follow one's conscience. Then one would act in the wrong way, as the conscience is mistaken. But how can one rightly go against the dictates of conscience? If one does, then one believes oneself to be acting wrongly, and one acts against the clear teaching that one should always obey one's conscience. The only escape from this dilemma is to deny the initial premise. It is in giving authority to conscience that the problem lies.[4]

Conscience is to be obeyed when properly instructed. But the emphasis of the work of moral decision-making should be placed elsewhere. The task of decision-making is to reason out what is right and wrong, where there is a moral choice. It does not help to claim conscience for such decisions; the work of conscience is best confined to instances where we know without risk of confusion what ought to be done, such as stealing from an unattended pile of coal!

Two strong developments in modern thought emphasise the importance of downplaying the role of conscience in the Christian life. Ironically, they point in opposite directions, since one insight points us to a suspicion of conscience, while the other exalts it. Psychologists since Freud have made clear how the formation of conscience in childhood can fall prey to arbitrary events and influences in early life. Guilt can just as easily be a negative feature of emotional development,

---

[3] C.S. Lewis supplies a sample list in his little book *The Abolition of Man*.

[4] See O'Donovan *Resurrection and Moral Order*, p. 117–18, for a discussion of this question.

as a positive spur to maturity. On the other hand, the reliance of modern individualism on personal decision making and personal sincerity and responsibility tends to give a very high place. Covenant ethics can learn from the psychological insight, in order to resist the exaggerated claims for personal moral choice.

Conscience: a third range of meaning

A third range of meaning also needs to be noted. The conscience played an important part in Sigmund Freud's psychology. He saw the conscience (or **superego**) as a significant aspect of our unconscious minds. Ever since then, without always accepting Freud's particular theories, we have been aware of the importance of the conscience as an emotional rather than rational element. We have emotional, almost instinctive reactions to the rightness or wrongness of some things, and these reactions are deeply formed by early childhood development. One person may have ineradicable feelings of guilt about trivial as well as important things. By contrast, other people feel little or no conscience about telling lies, or letting other people down, being late or fare-dodging. The strength and nature of our guilt feelings may bear very little relation to the moral seriousness (or otherwise) at issue. It is perhaps a little curious that our awareness of the psychological variability of our guilt feelings coexists in our culture with our conviction that conscience is the supreme moral judge.

Freud's theory of the 'superego' is not unchallenged, and no doubt does not provide a totally adequate and universal theory. But it remains sufficiently robust to give us good cause to suspect the doctrine of the authoritative conscience. According to Freud, the child learns to internalise the external authority figures they experience. As they grow up, they make the commands and reactions of this external authority their own. What is important about this view is that this is basically an emotional rather than a rational process. Various events or influences may make the superego respond strongly to particular areas. One person may grow up to feel guilty about spending money, another about sexual experience, another about dirt, another about loss of control through alcohol, untidiness, carelessness, etc. These emotions may well have a basis of some sort in morality; it is not good to be spendthrift, especially not with someone else's money, or to be sexually promiscuous or undisciplined. The point is that the emotions are hardly reliable guides to the seriousness or otherwise of such behaviour.

The problem cuts both ways. One person may have an exaggerated sense of the wrongness of something, which may easily have harmful moral effects in the opposite direction. Someone who feels guilty about ever spending money is going to find it difficult to respond appropriately to the needs of others, and will either give compulsively or perhaps not at all. On the other hand, someone else may have no guilt feelings at all in a particular area. Someone who feels no guilt about sexual engagement and emotions, and acts on that basis, may behave promiscuously and carelessly, leaving a trail of emotional damage.

Development of modern views of conscience

This brief analysis of the emotional development of guilt feelings, which can be quite normal, or absent, or exaggerated and pathological, is enough to warn us to be highly wary of giving too much authority to the conscience. Unfortunately, the devolution of moral authority to the individual which is so characteristic of modern life takes us in the opposite direction. To see how this is so dangerous, we should take up the analysis of Thomas Aquinas again, and see how things have progressed from there.

We recall that for Aquinas conscience could have two meanings — the inner prompting to obey known moral laws, or the faculty by which we discern the natural law. It is vital to realise that for Aquinas natural law is 'Rational participation in the eternal law'. The key word here is 'rational'. For Aquinas there was no question of a sort of instinctive or automatic understanding of morality. Natural law is a matter of reason, of careful thought. Of course Aquinas also recognised that people could reason to wrong conclusions, or that reason alone could not supply complete moral truth. Our reason is to be subject to God's revelation in scripture, though Aquinas believed that there was no question of a contradiction arising between reason and scripture. The problem that Aquinas asked 'Is it right to follow a mistaken conscience?' was for Aquinas only likely to occur quite rarely. The conscience should be fully instructed, subject to the reason and authority of the church's teaching. Modern secular thought, which adopts the doctrine of the duty always to obey one's conscience, takes leave of Aquinas' moral framework in two highly significant ways.

In modern secular individualism, Aquinas' emphasis on reason has been all but lost. All that remains of the conviction that it is only by careful reason and argument that one can discover moral truth is the view that one's moral choices should not be partial. Morality is only rational in the sense that it should not favour the self at the expense of others. It is therefore accepted that my moral choice cannot be that I have much more value than other people. I cannot morally realise my good at the cost of actively harming others. But many moral values are thus left open to personal choice (which is what modern individualism prizes above all else), whether determined emotionally, rationally, or in any other way. There is here no place from which we can criticise another person's conscientious moral choices, however bizarre or irrational they may seem, provided that they do not actively impinge on others to harm them.

At the same time, the modern conscience is not open to instruction. There is in principle no reason for it to be instructed, either by secular moral philosophy, or by religious moral belief. The doctrine of the sovereignty of the individual conscience indeed threatens to reduce morality to a minimal remnant. There is no good answer to be found on these terms to a whole variety of moral claims. The person who says that they have no responsibility to share their wealth with the needy; or the person who says that they have no responsibility for the emotional after-effects of their love affairs (since after all we are all adults); or the person who lives in an invented world of lies and fantasy. All these can, it would seem, be made claims which could be made more or less consistently, so that the person making them is happy for others to behave likewise. As such, it is hard to see what moral criticism can be made of such views, if the individual conscience is king. Clearly such a way of life is, in each case, less than Christian. But these distorted moral understandings, which are after all common enough in modern life, should illustrate the dangers of giving such authority to the conscience.

Nor are Christians exempt from such trends of thought. Protestants are convinced that they must make their own moral decisions. In

Veritatis Splendor John Paul II was at pains to tackle this question, as we have already seen. The encyclical agrees that moral behaviour always has an inward aspect, and that there is a creative aspect in thinking out the true moral course of action. 'Conscience is the *only* witness, since what takes place in the heart of the person is hidden from the eyes of everyone outside. Conscience makes its witness known only to the person himself. And, in turn, only the person himself knows what his own response is to the voice of conscience' (para. 57). 'The moral life calls for that creativity and originality typical of the person, the source and cause of his own deliberate acts' (para. 40). Elsewhere the Pope goes so far as to call the conscience the witness or even the voice of God (paras. 55, 58). However, it is clear, for the Pope, that the task of moral reason and discernment is always to be subject to the eternal law, the law of God.

Our whole discussion of conscience so far has been aimed at reducing and limiting its significance in moral discernment. It is time to pause and ask if the development of the concept is entirely on a downward path. What merit is there in the modern concern for freedom of conscience?

The conscience has a distinctive political role to play, and here the word conscience is used with reference to individual freedom. A clear example of the use of the word conscience in political life is in **conscientious objection** to military service. Here an individual claims the freedom not to be coerced into military service, on the grounds of personal conviction about the wrong of fighting and killing. It is one of the advantages of a democratic society that it is able to respect this conscientious conviction. But we ought to notice that this freedom to dissent is based on a reasoned (and respected) tradition within Christianity — it is not merely an emotional reaction or a personal preference. In valuing freedom of conscience very highly, we ask that those who conscientiously dissent from those in authority engage critically and rationally, giving good reasons for their dissent.

The modern emphasis on individual moral responsibility particularly needs to recognise that morality is rational. This rationality is founded on a theological basis, and our personal decisions have to be rightly situated in such a framework. In order to fill out the positive place, or proper understanding of conscience, in the Christian life, we should look at some examples.

Conscience at Work

In order to maintain some continuity of theme, we will take some examples of the place of conscience in the handling of money and property. We begin with an example of the simplest, and most proper, activity of the conscience.

In my college library it is easy to borrow a book without signing it out. To do this can be very convenient, saving time when I am in a hurry, or allowing me to keep the book as long as I like without worrying about the recall date. Or perhaps I have it in mind not to return the book but to keep it. There can be no question that it is right for me to follow the library rules, to borrow the book only when I have signed it out. Here it would be the proper activity of my conscience to warn me against breaking the rules, or to make me feel guilty if I did break them, with the effect of prompting me to return the book forthwith. There is nothing problematic here. The sense of inner pain which we call guilt is the original sense of conscience used in the New Testament, following Greek usage. Conscience makes me feel bad when I have done something I know quite clearly I ought not to do.

But conscience can also make me feel bad when I do something which is not wrong. Some people, for instance, feel guilty about spending money on anything which is not essential. Of course, there is extravagance which is morally blameworthy, in a world of need. But the refusal to enjoy good food on occasion, and the convivial company of friends and family, can amount to a refusal to enjoy the goodness of God's blessings. It is not wrong to balance the money we spend for ourselves with the money we give away to provide for the needy. Our task is to consider carefully how to strike the right balance, and to allow our conscience to be instructed by rational thought. Our feelings of guilt arise from the emotional effects of our upbringing, or perhaps from experience of times when extravagance actually threatened the ability to provide for basic needs. Such guilt feelings can make us err in another direction, in being so parsimonious and mean that we fail to offer hospitality as we should.

On the other hand, many people feel no guilt at all at spending their money freely on their own wants and desires, without any thought for those who are in need. The lack of any sense of guilt in personal extravagance does not thereby justify such use of money. Just as the naturally tender of conscience need to educate their conscience, so do those who have a more robust conscience. In either case the task is to think through the appropriate balance and approach. The extravagant person needs to consider their duty to use their money for the common good. We can recall here that the right to private property carries with it the duty to use that property for the good of others. The Christian view of private property rights does not accept that I have complete moral freedom to use all my property simply as I choose, without regard for others.

Both the over-scrupulous and the thick-skinned need to ensure that their conscience is instructed and educated, the one to reduce the guilt, the other not to rely on its absence. Either way, our inner emotions do not carry authority over our moral decisions.

We could give another example of the way conscience is used, again in relation to the management of money. The popularity of ethical investment funds is growing. Such approaches to investment in the stock market take account of a variety of factors in deciding what shares to invest in. These typically include avoiding arms, tobacco, alcohol, and may also examine employment and environmental policies along with other aspects of a company's conduct. A manager of such funds is faced with a variety of decisions about what investment is to be considered ethically acceptable. Such a manager might say that in finely balanced judgements there was no hard and fast rule, but that in each case they 'Followed their conscience'. By this they mean that there can be no moral certainty in all cases and in the end they have to rely on a trained intuition, a matter of personal weighing of contrasting factors to arrive at a decision.

In this kind of instance, the word conscience is used to describe the operation of a well-trained intuition or professional judgement. It is important to notice that decisions made in this way, though clearly moral decisions, and clearly made by the individual in a way that might differ from the approach of someone equally upright and skilled, are nevertheless based on a clear apprehension of a moral framework. There is no guarantee that we can know with certainty the right thing to do in such positions, or indeed that there is a clear moral right and wrong. It does not seem, however, that it is helpful to call the process of personal judgement on such occasions the operation of conscience. Surely such individual discernments rest on a mixture of understanding, skill, insight and intuition. The word conscience is best reserved for occasions when guilt is aroused as a result of contravening a clear moral precept.

A case like this leads to our final example, which offers a case where the use of a 'clear conscience' simply enables someone to feel justified in doing something that is simply wrong. Let us suppose someone who believes that income tax is a form of theft, which however legal, deprives the taxpayer of their rightfully earned property. Up to a point, such a person cannot avoid paying the tax. But suppose also that they find some way of evading the tax, which they objectively know to be against the law, but which they are confident that they can get away with. Their 'conscience' (i.e. at this point, their moral reason) balances up the conflicting feelings that the tax itself is unjustifiable and it is nevertheless right to obey the law. But then their conscience (i.e feelings of guilt, or lack of them) might very well provide no indication that tax evasion is wrong. In evading the tax, they feel no guilt as a result. The work of thinking through what ought to be done is given the name conscience. Here the faculty of conscience as the faculty whereby we apprehend the natural law is confused with the emotion of guilt which is the proper response to having done something wrong.

It is time for Christian moral teaching to be much more cautious about the authority of conscience. The danger of saying that we should always follow our conscience is that it plays into the hand of the individualist approach to morality, where each person must make their own free choice of values, and try to pursue them consistently. It is true that we should obey our conscience, as St Paul taught. But the conscience must be properly instructed. The 'conscience' simply cannot actually teach us the content of morality. All it can do is recall us to our duty to obey moral instruction. There are, in addition, many moral decisions which are properly a matter of individual decision. But it is not helpful to call such decisions a matter of conscience — they are matters of moral choice, moral decision, moral judgement.

Fourteen

Christian Moral Witness

How may Christian morality be best commended in our day? On the face of it, it looks as if clear explanation of Christian morality should be much in demand. There are many calls for the churches to teach and commend moral principles, in a day when morality seems increasingly to be confused or ignored. The sense of change brings its own reaction, as some people look for security, a knowledge of reliable values.

Neither the sense of being confused, nor the worried reaction to confusion, provides a good basis for moral understanding. But there are also reasons why the moral framework we have sketched here does not fit very easily into contemporary calls for moral renewal. Partly this is because people are not on the whole looking for a framework for morality. Perhaps they have given up thinking that a moral framework is possible, as we are committed to a variety of moral values (as if we have a number of scattered signposts, but no map). More seriously, many are concerned that the search for a framework of truth will be divisive or sectarian. So there are problems in the church offering moral teaching. Many who want to hear a moral lead want to hear only the morality; they may not want to hear the church's religious teaching. Of course there are many who don't want to hear the church's moral teaching at all, with or without the explicitly religious aspects. Nor must one discount the cynic's observation that we usually want other people to be morally educated, not ourselves. It's a bit like listening to a sharply-aimed sermon and thinking of all one's friends who particularly need to hear it!

So a number of questions are raised. If Christians make claims about the truth of Christian morality, is that acceptable in a pluralist society?

Claims to moral truth are often said to be imperialistic, because any claim to truth is seen as little more than a concealed power claim. This question is obviously a relevant one when we consider the issue of legislation. For the establishment and enforcement of laws is obviously a matter of power. Is it right, therefore, for Christians to seek to have their views of moral truth enforced by political power? Here we unavoidably enter the discussion about the way morality relates to legislation. Several considerations have to be taken into account. True moral behaviour is a matter of free conscientious action, so it is clearly right for the law to value personal liberty. There is a widespread view (stemming from John Stuart Mill) that moral views are not a good basis for legislation; the main, or only purpose of laws is to prevent people from being harmed. In considering public **moral witness**, then, we need to have a good understanding of the purpose of law. We need to consider how far law can be used to inculcate good moral practice, at what point one has to hold back from legislating moral convictions, and generally how important it is for Christians to be involved in the processes of political power, with its inevitable compromises and concessions.

There are a number of options for the church's public witness. To a large extent the course the church follows must depend on its situation in society, its own strength and the attitudes of society. The extent to which the church attempts to influence or form the shape of society is more a matter of tactics than strategy. There can be no general blueprint. At times the church may be a small group, to whom nobody particularly wishes to listen. Then the church's witness must consist mainly of its way of life, its example, rather than its speech. At another extreme, society may be largely Christian, and look to the church to provide moral instruction, willing to hear that on an explicitly religious basis. In such societies, of course, the church has to take care not to be dazzled by earthly power, which is in any case always likely to be in contention. The church must beware that it does not confuse its own inner faith with what can be established in law. More often, and certainly in our day, the situation is somewhere between these two. The church can do more than give an example, for its voice is certainly heard on some levels; on the other hand there are aspects of its witness which do not receive a willing hearing. So it needs to be clear about the distinction between its inner life, and what it succeeds in establishing in social terms.

Our discussion of the church's witness centres on 'law and morality', and on the priorities for public moral witness. This is a much debated area, and we can only give a brief outline, using particular examples to illustrate the general questions. We focus on it because it is important in its own right, but it must be emphasised that it is only one aspect of the church's moral witness. There are several other aspects, and these include the church's own moral life and self-discipline, its moral teaching, as well as its witness on specific social questions (one thinks of unemployment or third world debt, for example).

Law and Morality

To attempt to clarify the strategy for Christian moral witness by turning to the much discussed topic of the relationship of law and morality may seem unpromising. The law is the scene of a confused and contentious struggle, with everyone arguing past each other from a variety of assumptions with many different goals. We are delivered into debates about detail, about what is or is not factually true, and we are never able to start from an ideal situation. There are all sorts of factors to be taken into account. There is a balance to be struck between seeking the common good and allowing individual and group liberties. We have to protect people from harm, yet there are all sorts of ways of deciding what is to count as harm. We have to balance the desirability of influencing social behaviour by using the law as an educator, against the risk of losing respect for the law if people are not convinced in their own minds about the moral points at issue. In reforming particular laws, it has also to be borne in mind that it is not only the substance of the reform, but its perception and general direction, which may be just as important. (A good deal of the debate about the government's proposals for divorce law reform (1995–6) has more to do with how the reforms will be perceived than the actual substance of the reform. In particular, many fear that shifting the emphasis away from offence draws attention to the ease with which people can ignore their marriage commitment.)

Oliver O'Donovan has offered a valuable clarification of these questions.[1] He suggests that legislation needs to be based on three considerations. One point is that the law must be based on a sense of what is morally right. In particular, O'Donovan expresses this as 'the claim of the injured's right to be avenged'. If people do not see the law as based on a sense of justice, of correcting and preventing injustice, then they will lose respect for it. 'People obey political authority because they think they ought'.[2] For instance, it seems to be a matter of justice that the law should try to protect those who want to remain faithful to their marriage, against the arbitrary decision of one partner to seek a divorce. There should, we feel, be legal safeguards for the wife who is abandoned by her husband in favour of someone perhaps younger, fresher, more attractive to him. A second point is that legislation must reflect and embody the accepted traditions which form society, and which hold it together. In a country where the majority are churchgoers, it may be quite unproblematic to maintain legal restrictions on Sunday activities. Such laws restrict what a few people may wish to do, but on the whole they express the community's beliefs that Sunday is to be honoured in a special way. The third point is the obvious one that legislation rests on power, and must be enforced by effective action. This has real implications for many areas of law. One classic example is that of the failure of prohibition (laws against alcohol). Prohibition laws became unenforceable, and led to the flourishing of criminality on a large scale. A similar motive lies behind permissive abortion laws. One reason for allowing abortions to be performed legally is the fear of illegal 'back-street' abortions, with their attendant health risks.[3]

O'Donovan's framework is helpful in locating the areas which must not be overlooked. Let us begin with the view that the essential criterion for legislation is that it should prevent harm.

---

[1] See *Ressurrection and Moral Order*, pp. 97, 127–30.

[2] Ibid., p. 128.

[3] Anti-abortion campaigners believe this fear to be greatly exaggerated. The debate about illegal abortions before the law was reformed turns on hugely varied statistics — all little better than educated guesses!

Putting things right

At first sight the criterion of preventing harm is attractive, since it provides a simple and powerful means of agreement, while at the same time offering the greatest individual liberty.[4] J.S. Mill provides the classic statement: 'The only purpose for which power can be rightfully exercised over any member of a civilised community against his will is to prevent harm to others. His own good, either physical or moral, is not a sufficient warrant'.[5] There can be little doubt that this powerful criterion has been and remains enormously influential. But, as Lee points out, there are in fact several unanswered questions. What constitutes harm? Who is to count as a subject of harm? (Does the fetus count, for instance? Or animals?) Can society really not promote people's own good, and prevent them from harming themselves? Lee establishes convincingly that Mill's principle is less simple and effective than it appears at first sight. Yet the principle does seem to need taking into account.

O'Donovan's point about the avenging of injured right helps to focus the criterion of harm to others. The reason why we pass laws to punish those who do harm to others is fundamentally because a wrong is done when someone is deliberately harmed. (There are occasions when harm is deliberately done, but there is no wrong, such as competitive boxing.) The fact that we debate how strictly to frame laws to limit the possibilities of harm in such sports also shows that 'harm to others' is not the sole criterion. Here our concern is for the good of the boxers concerned, however willingly they take the risk of being harmed. In a similar way we pass laws to try to limit or deter the use of such things as tobacco, drugs and alcohol, by which people can harm themselves, sometimes without harming others in any direct way. The criterion of harm turns out after all to be a moral criterion, and does not offer a way to escape debates about what moral beliefs should be enshrined in legislation.

One suggestion for distinguishing which moral convictions should give rise to laws is the difference between public and private behaviour. Should we only legislate on matters concerning the

---

[4] For a very helpful account of this subject, see Simon Lee, *Law and Morals*, on which I have drawn here.

[5] Mill, *On Liberty*, cited by Lee, p. 22.

public good, while leaving private behaviour as an area of freedom? This looks an attractive idea, but the distinction cannot be drawn in a watertight way. For instance, sexual behaviour may appear a private matter, but it is rarely only a private matter. If two young people make love, then that would seem to be their concern, and theirs alone. If however the woman conceives a child, then that is already a public matter, for the child will not be their child only, but will be part of a wider family and community.[6] Society, then, does have an interest in preventing sexual harm. At times it pursues this interest by legislation, in particular to protect marriage. Society also expresses its concern in customary practices, ceremonies, rituals and unwritten prohibitions. Without this basis in custom, indeed, it is hard to see how any laws about marriage and the family can provide the needed restraints all on their own. (There are further reasons why it is wise to limit legislation in this area, which have to do with the law's effectiveness.)

Moral Agreement

O'Donovan's framework for understanding the basis for legislation points out that laws must reflect and embody a society's traditions, especially its agreements about morality. Legislation cannot afford to be too far away from the community's shared convictions about what is right. Particularly in the modern age where society is in a chronic state of perpetual change, our shared moral convictions are continually liable to shift. **Pornography** provides a fair example of this. The difficulty with maintaining obscenity laws is quite simply that over the last twenty years, let alone the last fifty, many people have been prepared to offer moral defences for things which would previously have been morally unthinkable. And among those who personally consider pornography morally undesirable, many are not convinced that it is a matter of injustice. The evidence as to whether pornography

---

[6] The concern for children is not the only, or the most central aspect, of society's interest in sexual behaviour. Our sexual relationships, after all, are one of the most influential of the ways in which people interact; and this has far-reaching implications for any society or organisation. The way society regulates sexual relationships is fundamental to the whole shape of that society. Cf. also S. Hauerwas, *A Community of Character*, chs. 8–10.

tends to lead people to aggressive sexual acts against others cannot be said to be conclusive.

While laws often have to follow the changing moral agreements of society, they can also play an important part in forming our moral consensus. **Race discrimination** laws in Britain have a mixed history. On the one hand it is not hard to point to persistent racist feelings and activities. The law has not been sufficient to overcome deeply held views and prejudices. On the other hand, it is also true that many people have reviewed their attitudes and practices in the light of the law, and it seems a plausible claim that the Race Relations Act has been a significant element in leading to a different moral climate. Another hotly debated issue shows that a moral point of view can influence public justice, in spite of the differing moral views of the majority. There is clearly a majority in favour of the return of capital punishment as the sentence for certain crimes. This majority is allied to the attitude that wants much severer prison sentences for many serious crimes. In the face of these views, Parliament has been consistent over a generation in its moral opposition to capital punish-ment, and generally to more punitive forms of sentencing. It has been convinced that it is its duty to try to lead public opinion, not merely to follow it.

With these thoughts in mind, we can consider two areas where Christians have urged their own moral convictions. In debates about **abortion**, and about **Sunday trading**, Christians have had to try to estimate where they could appeal to an existing moral consensus, where they could persuade public opinion, and where they had to recognise that the moral ethos simply did not accept Christian beliefs. Our society has no very clear view about the rights and wrongs of abortion. Whereas most people see it as an evil, a majority sees it as one evil to be weighed against others. Hence the prevalent view that each particular case should be a matter for the decision of the woman concerned. In the USA it is explicit that the important moral principle at stake is the personal freedom of the (potential) mother to make her own choice. Against this, the Christian can only protest that the unborn child is in fact a human being, worthy of our protection. One can only wonder, as the debate continues, how long it will take for increasing awareness of the reality of human life in the womb to affect public perceptions. The widespread use of ultrasound scans shows very graphically the hidden growth and humanity of the unborn child. It is only when people recognise the true nature of what happens in 'termination of pregnancy' that it will be possible to pass more restrictive legislation on abortion. A change in moral perceptions here needs to precede legal reform. In this light, one wonders about Christian campaigns about the margins of abortion law, such as trying to reduce the maximum age of gestation for legal abortions. Such campaigns sometimes seem to imply that abortion is less blameworthy if done at 12 weeks rather than 16, or 16 weeks rather than 20. Such distinctions can have very little substance. One danger of stating or implying them may be to blur the central contention that any unborn child is essentially a new human being.

If the consensus view on abortion is strongly in favour of its continuing legality, opinion on Sunday trading is much nearer to being equally divided. Many wish to observe Sunday in some way, just as there are those who want to have the maximum freedom every day of the week. In public debates over the last few years, British law remained for a while quite restrictive on Sunday trading. More recently the government has been able to pass much more liberal laws to permit Sunday trading, though it remains limited at the present time. It has to be admitted that one of the genuine problems faced by Parliament was the disrespect with which the old laws were treated. The evidence of people's wishes, as given in their behaviour, was that retailers and shoppers alike wished to shop on Sundays, and that local authorities were reluctant to enforce the law. To some extent the law has to enshrine what is publicly believed to be right, for it cannot always be instructing an unwilling audience. If this is true, it is also the case that changing the law also has an effect in changing people's perceptions and behaviour.

The Enforcement of Law

The third point in O'Donovan's framework is that laws are matters for enforcement. This point, which appears at first sight simply to be a pragmatic question, actually has significant implications for the nature of law. We can examine some of these by looking at questions of **ecology** and **environmental damage**. We can begin by agreeing that there are some matters of pollution that everyone would wish to see controlled, subject to legal sanctions. Some already are, such as deliberate dumping of poisonous chemicals, or the spilling of oil wastes at sea. There is a clear consensus that such things should be controlled, and, as a matter of justice, it is clear that deliberate polluting is morally wrong. However, there are further questions about extending the scope of legislation. First, there has to be effective power to get laws passed. Second, when laws are passed, they have to be drafted so as to make enforcement possible, and effective enforcement is essential. This can be problematic, thirdly, when enforcement is a global matter. There is a need for international action to agree, create and enforce workable laws.

Legislation depends on the active use of power. In many ecological concerns many people may have a real economic interest. Not everyone wants to pay in order to express their respect for the natural world. It is not only car manufacturers who do not want petrol to be taxed even more heavily, but everyone who drives a car. It is not only power generators who are reluctant to clean up emissions from power stations, but everyone who pays the resulting electricity bills. Economic power can be exercised by lobbies for the car industry, the oil industry, the power industry, and so on. But it is also true that no proposal which will raise prices will be welcome in a democratic economy. If we believe that ecological concern is a moral priority, it is necessary to persuade people to be ready to pay for such concern.

Taking this point seriously may also mean a radical re-examination of the way we calculate economic success. In traditional economics, there are 'external costs' which are not usually paid.[7] Economic calculations, which are apparently morally neutral, can be matters of great moral significance. The operation of markets, the handling of money, the effects of the 'Law of supply and demand', all these can result in the effective use of power. Such use of power can be concealed, not only from outsiders, but also from those who have the power bestowed on them by the operation of the market. For instance, those who consume electricity, natural gas, and so on, for cooking,

---

[7] See, for example, D. Hay, *Economics Today*, pp. 285–308.

heating and a myriad of other uses may well be benefiting from processes which inflict cumulative damage on nature. The burning of fossil fuels uses up limited resources, and adds to the 'greenhouse' effect which leads to global warming. So the consumer benefits by a system which is doing great potential damage. But the consumer pays little if anything for the costs of using scarce resources, and increasing atmospheric levels of carbon dioxide (a major 'greenhouse' gas). If there is a political will to reduce the damage done by overuse of fuel, it will have to be expressed in an economic way.

Any law has to be able to be enforced. This is why few societies have ever tried to put legal controls on sex outside marriage, however wrong they have believed it to be. Shakespeare's play *Measure for Measure* explores the moral and human consequences of passing such laws, which turn out to be quite unjust in operation.[8] The prohibition of alcohol in the United States provided a similar example. The implications of this point for controlling ecological damage are clear. On the one hand, a sufficient proportion of the population has to see proper controls as warranted and fair, if they are to be acceptable. Laws which protect particular areas of land, or particular species, and so on, need to be held in respect or they will simply be flouted. On the other hand, it may be much better to impose taxes in some matters, rather than directly regulating against abuse or excess. It may be better to increase the tax on petrol than trying to stop people driving cars which are wasteful and excessively polluting.

There are some kinds of ecological damage which are clearly global rather than local. Global warming, holes in the ozone layer, pollution of the oceans, destruction of forests, loss of species, are all concerns which have to be tackled on an international scale. Pope John XXIII, writing in 1963,[9] argued from this that a world political authority is necessary. Other theologians have been concerned about this, fearing the dangers of entrusting global power to any human institution. Lutherans in particular tend to be concerned that any human authority needs to be checked by countervailing authorities.[10] Quite a lot can be achieved by global bodies with particular specialist concerns. One

---

[8] The behaviour of the judge is not the only problem; the play makes clear that it is the law itself which helps to cause the trouble.

[9] In the encyclical *Pacem in Terris*.

[10] See for instance Helmut Thielicke, *Theological Ethics 2: Politics*.

example of such action is the eradication of smallpox under the aegis of the World Health Organisation. It is doubtful, though, that such organisations could effectively challenge established political or economic interests. The International Whaling Commission has found it very difficult to check the interests of particular nations in their own whaling industries. Another way forward is to gain specific ad hoc agreements, such as those on the use of CFCs. Here again, the difficulty is gaining an effective worldwide agreement.

The path of Christian moral witness

Our discussion of the relation between morality and the law has pointed to some of the dimensions of Christian moral witness. In pressing for legislative action, Christians have to recognise not only the moral basis for their viewpoint, but also the degree of fit between their viewpoint and the consensus, if any, of the whole community. In legislation, the dimension of effective power and enforcement has also to be considered.

The concern to affect legislation is not the whole of Christian moral witness. One of the main arguments of this book has been that true moral beliefs are an integral part of Christian beliefs. Those beliefs are true, and they are good for everyone. Christian morality is good news for the hearer who takes the message to heart, just as much as the knowledge of forgiveness, of redemption, and so on. Christian moral teaching should be an integral part of all Christian teaching. There is no need to apologise for being convinced about moral truth, or for the fact that it depends on Christian faith. It is not all that long since much moral belief could be taken for granted by Christian teaching and preaching. However, the challenge now is to explain the rationale behind moral beliefs; and to be clear that Christian moral perspectives have different foundations from value-based moralities, (those based purely on the individual conscience making its own arrangement of a series of moral values).

Another major argument of the book has been the recognition that morality is in principle no simpler than the created realities with which it deals. For example, the morality of truth-telling has to acknowledge the way that truth-telling belongs within human relationships. Usually our relationships should be straightforward and open, but there can be good reasons why this is not so. This is not quibbling, but accuracy. The effort to dispel moral confusion and cynicism cannot afford to be impatient with such questions, as refusal to handle genuine difficulties is as damaging in its way as believing that all morality is problematic.

Christian moral witness must, then, emphasise reason and explanation. The clarification of what is right and wrong, good and bad, must be the priority. At the same time this must, self-evidently, be put forward in relation to the moral beliefs and frameworks of others. Christians do not need to shy away from agreement with people of other persuasions, nor do they have to find unanimity with them at all points. Identifying what it is that makes up the current moral consensus (if any) is by no means easy. The more Christians can identify with such consensus, and move it along, the more they will feel that their service to the community is in making such views the acknowledged views of society. Endeavouring to frame, or maintain, just and good laws for society is part of service to that society. As we have seen, doing this means entering into the struggle for political power. But the prior task must always be the clarification of what Christians themselves actually believe.

Four Examples

To see what this might mean, we will briefly survey four current debates: abortion, divorce law, Sunday trading, and ecology.

a) Abortion

A very substantial proportion of human conceptions in the developed countries of the world are presently terminated by abortion.[11] The increased availability of contraception, together with efforts to improve sex education, seems to have done little to prevent people from conceiving unwanted babies. Increased emphasis on personal autonomy has gone alongside an increasing awareness of the facts about the growth of the fetus in the womb. At the same time, hospitals daily witness the irony of performing abortions of perfectly healthy babies

---

[11] Typically, there may be one abortion to every two or three births. In Britain about 180,000 abortions are performed each year. Annual figures are to be found in HMSO's *Social Trends*.

while struggling to help others who desperately want children but are unable to have their own without assistance. Few babies are put up for adoption, mainly because of the emphasis on the great desirability of mothers being able to bring up their own children.

Meanwhile Christians are divided in their own responses. The reasons originally given for abortion law reform stressed the distinction between law and morality. It was argued that prohibiting abortion led to dangerous illegal abortions, and that a strict law against abortion prevented people from making their own responsible choices. Liberal reform, it was said, did not imply anything about the morality or otherwise of abortion. Conscience clauses were enshrined in the law to allow medical staff not to participate if they believed abortion to be wrong. However, such clauses have been of limited effect. In addition, changes to the law have had a significant effect on perceptions about morality.

In this situation, Christians wishing to convince others of the sanctity of the unborn child's life have adopted a number of strategies. Firstly, and fundamentally, they have continued to try to persuade others of the moral truth they hold. Arguments can be found in the Bible, in Christian tradition and theology,[12] and in the vivid knowledge of hidden growth which can be obtained by modern photographic and pictorial means. The attempt to persuade must surely remain the essential emphasis of such campaigning. More practical strategies have also been adopted. In North America, some have resorted to violent direct action. Such protestors have argued there are few limits to be placed on attempts to save life. Not only are their protests likely to be counterproductive, they make the more fundamental error of believing that one can bring about good by doing evil.[13] Another practical strategy has been to try to alter the detailed limits on the legality of abortion, in particular the maximum age for a legal abortion. But the most convincing thing Christians do in

---

[12] See, for instance, *Abortion and the Sanctity of Human Life*, J.H. Channer (ed.) for a representative collection of essays.

[13] There is a much more intricate discussion here about the reasons why such protests cannot find justification in the Just War tradition about the use of force. It is within that tradition that one can examine the moral purposes and limits of civil disobedience. See article 'Civil Disobedience' in *New Dictionary of Christian Ethics and Pastoral Theology*, D. Atkinson and D. Field (eds.).

support of their 'pro-life' convictions is to provide practical support to mothers who need it. As Hauerwas has written 'If we do not give our resources, our money . . . to support these young women, then we have no right to stand by self-righteously and point to them saying 'Sorry. Tough luck. Abortion is a sin. It is your problem'.[14]

b) *Divorce law*

As far as abortion is concerned, there is substantial agreement about the wrongness of abortion. Disagreements among theologians concern what circumstances might justify abortion (such as saving the mother's life or health, rape, etc.), not the fact that life in the womb should be protected. There is much greater diversity over the morality of divorce. While everyone agrees that marriage should be permanent, many believe that divorce and remarriage can never be right, while many others see such a course as potentially the right one. There are substantial reasons and arguments on almost all sides of the issue. The declared stance of the Church of England, and its day-to-day practice, is confused and confusing. Christians can and do enter the debates about divorce law reform, but it is hard to see that the Church can make any very distinctive contribution at this level, partly because of its own confusion and lack of agreement, and partly because of the technical legal problems of framing workable laws.

There can be little doubt that Christian witness to the importance of marriage must be an acted rather than a spoken witness. Marriage preparation, marriage counselling, marriage enrichment, all are ways of helping people to learn how and why marriages can be strengthened. At the same time, an emphasis on marriage needs to go along with the Christian perspective that marriage is not the be-all and end-all. There is a place for single people, possibly a more exalted place (if we are to take Jesus at his word). There is also a place for those whose marriages have failed, for marriage failure is not the unforgivable sin. Here are real tensions, but they are tensions which can be lived with more than they can be solved in theory. Perhaps the most significant point to be made here is that one thing makes both marriage and singleness more difficult, and that is the idea of a perfect

---

[14] Paraphrasing an appeal by Jerry Falwell for support of 'Save a Baby Homes', *Resident Aliens*, Stanley Hauerwas and William H. Willimon.

marriage. Our society places so much weight on what we expect from marriage, that it is not surprising that it gives way under the strain; and such expectations also devalue being single.

c)   Sunday trading

It is often taken for granted that the nature of Sunday observance is made perfectly clear in the Bible. However, this is to assume too much. First, of course, the Old Testament Sabbath is a Jewish, not a Christian, custom. Christians changed the Sabbath day to Sunday. Moreover, parts of the New Testament seriously question the meaning and observance of a special day. Jesus pointed out that 'The Sabbath was made for man, not man for the Sabbath'.[15] Paul seemed to regard the keeping of special days as a legitimate matter for local conviction. And the writer to the Hebrews sees the significance of the Sabbath as being a symbol of the heavenly rest.

Karl Barth pointed out that one important implication of the Sabbath rest is that it limits our daily work.[16] Perhaps it is more important for Christians to say that our society's hopes and wishes are too much placed on economic success. Our concern to work, to make things, to do things, to make money, threatens to take over our whole lives. The point about Sunday is that we stop getting, spending, and chasing an unreal and unrealisable dream. Is it good that we should worship money everyday? Should we not find our real selves? Here are some of the questions which the Sabbath command puts to our frenetic society. If people are not even willing to hear such questions, then it is all the more important for Christians to continue to answer them in their lives.

d)   Ecological concern

Concern for the environment has to be taken seriously. Two different kinds of reasons are often given for this. If we speak of concern for the **environment**, we draw attention to the fact that the world is gradually being made less hospitable for the supporting of life, especially human life. If the world heats up by two or three degrees, it is

---

[15] Mark 2:27
[16] *Church Dogmatics*, III, iv, pp. 66–72, 550–55.

almost certain that there would be big changes in the climate. Sea levels would rise, threatening the many cities and peoples who live at or near sea level. Climate change could have a serious effect on current food production; for instance rainfall patterns will be altered. The world's environment for human life would be much changed. One kind of reason for concern, then, is the dangers and losses caused to human populations, to human welfare.

If we speak of **ecological** concern, we transfer our attention to the natural world for its own sake. A world without tigers, or pandas, or dolphins, would only be a slightly diminished world so far as human welfare is concerned. Indeed the extinction of tigers in the wild would make some places safer for human beings. But tigers, dolphins, and the myriads of other threatened species, are all part of God's created world. As such they deserve respect in their own right, quite apart from their contribution to human life.

Both kinds of reason are compelling in their own right. On the whole, I suspect, more emphasis is placed on environmental arguments, the concern for human welfare, than on respect for nature as such. It is an open question which kind of argument is more effective in persuading people to change their way of life and their attitudes. However, it may be that it is more fundamental to say that God's world should be respected, than to say that humanity is putting itself at risk. One reason for this is that human beings have almost boundless self-confidence in being able to adapt to new challenges. Threats of future danger may not prove compelling, for this reason. Twenty years ago, there were many predictions of oil reserves being exhausted. But new reserves were discovered, so it is now believed that they will last out the lifetime of everyone presently alive. The threat has receded, leading, perhaps, to fresh complacency. Future danger may not be a persuasive motive, or a clear moral reason for action.

To speak of respect for what God has made is a clear reason for present action. There can be no doubt that the Bible speaks of an attitude of respect for nature. Of course there is a debate about what exactly respect means. Nature is not God, and human beings have responsibility for the earth. Humanity stands in a special relationship to the world, to care for it and to use it. A great deal needs to be done to see what this means for human technology and industry. What sort of limits should be placed on technological invention and adaptation? How should we calculate economic success in a way that treats nature with proper respect, and doesn't just see the natural world as a resource? The only way in which these huge questions, and others like them, can be properly considered, is by looking at what we are actually doing here and now, not merely by trying to work out future possibilities for disaster.

In each of these four areas of current debate, two themes have emerged. One is that each of them demands careful thought and reason. Our world is continually asking new questions about old traditions, and about new possibilities. Old answers and formulations cannot be taken for granted. In thinking through contemporary responses, there is much to learn from the Christian tradition. But the tradition must be thought through and made relevant.

Another feature of our world is that it seems to be growing increasingly uncertain of the hope of seeing things whole. Debates are reduced to scattered sound bites for and against. Does this mean that a book like this, which has tried to set out a framework for seeing things whole, is out of date?

The answer to this question comes in two parts. In the first place, Christians have a continuing duty to maintain their witness to the truth. Of course it is right to gain a hearing for Christian witness. But it is more important to remain truthful, than to adapt what is said purely so that it will be heard. When the king of Judah refused to hear Jeremiah's message and systematically burned it, Jeremiah simply went and dictated it all again.[17]

The second part of the answer, and the common theme of all Christian moral witness, is that Christian witness is to be lived out, not just spoken. Action, whether finally effective or not, is just as much a witness as the words that are written or spoken. At the heart of this witness is the Christian love, to be expressed in word and deed.

'And now I give you a new commandment: love one another. As I have loved you, so you must love one another. If you have love for one another, then everyone will know that you are my disciples.'[18]

---

[17] Jeremiah 36, esp. v. 32.
[18] John 13:34–35.

Bibliography

Adams, R., *Watership Down*, (Harmondsworth, Penguin 1973)

Almond, B., 'Seven Moral Myths', *Philosophy* 65 (1990), pp. 129–136; also reprinted in Rodd, C.S. (ed.), *New Occasions Teach New Duties?* (Edinburgh, T&T Clark 1995)

Atkinson, D. and Field, D., *New Dictionary of Christian Ethics and Pastoral Theology*, (Leicester, IVP 1995), *see* 'Civil Disobedience'

Attwood, D., *Paul Ramsey's Political Ethics*, (Lanham, Maryland, Rowman and Littlefield 1992)

Barth, K., *Church Dogmatics* III, i and III, iv, (Edinburgh, T&T Clark 1958, 1961)

Bellah, R.N. et al., *Habits of the Heart*, (Berkeley, University of California Press 1985)

Brett, P., *Love Your Neighbour*, (London, DLT 1992)

Cameron, N.M. de S., *The New Medicine*, (London, Hodder and Stoughton 1991)

Channer, J.H. (ed.), *Abortion and the Sanctity of Life*, (Exeter, Paternoster 1985)

Cornes, A., *Divorce and Remarriage*, (London, Hodder and Stoughton 1993)

Donne, J., *Selected Prose*, (Harmondsworth, Penguin 1987)

Dworkin, R., *Life's dominion: An Argument about Abortion and Euthanasia*, (London, HarperCollins 1993)

Ellul, J., *The Technological Society*, J. Wilkinson (tr.) (London, Jonathan Cape 1965)

Giddens, A., *The Consequences of Modernity*, (Cambridge, Polity Press 1990)

Gormally, L. (ed.), *Euthanasia, Clinical Practice and the Law*, (London, The Linacre Centre for Health Care Ethics 1994)

HMSO, *Social Trends 1997* (etc.), (London, The Stationery Office, annually)

Harvey, A., *Promise or Pretence?*, (London, SCM 1994)

Harvey, A., *Strenuous Commands: The Ethic of Jesus*, (London, SCM 1990)

Hauerwas, S., *A Community of Character*, (Notre Dame, University of Notre Dame Press 1981)

Hauerwas, S., *The Peacable Kingdom*, (London, SCM 1984)

Hauerwas, S., and Willimon, W.H., *Resident Aliens*, (Nashville, Abingdon 1989)

Hauerwas, S., *Truthfulness and Tragedy*, (Notre Dame, University of Notre Dame Press 1977)

Hay, D., *Economics Today*, (Leicester, Apollos 1989)

Illich, I., *Deschooling Society*, (Harmondsworth, Penguin 1971)

Illich, I., *Limits to Medicine*, (Harmondsworth, Penguin 1976)

Illich, I., *Gender*, (London, Marion Boyars 1983)

Keeling, M., *The Foundations of Christian Ethics*, (Edinburgh, T&T Clark 1990)

Keown, J., 'Courting Euthanasia?: Tony Bland and the Law Lords', *Ethics and Medicine* 9/3 (Autumn 1993), pp. 34–7

King, M.L., *Strength to Love*, (London, Hodder and Stoughton 1963)

Lee, S., *Law and Morals*, (Oxford, OUP 1986)

Lewis, C.S., *The Abolition of Man*, (London, Fount 1978)

Linacre Centre, *Euthanasia and Clinical Practice: trends, principles and alternatives*, (London, Linacre Centre 1982), *see also* Gormally, L., *Euthanasia*

Luther, M., 'The Freedom of a Christian' in, for instance, Dillenberger, J. (ed.), *Martin Luther: Selections from his writings*, (Anchor Books 1961)

McDonald, I., *Christian Values: Theory and Practice in Christian Ethics Today*, (Edinburgh, T&T Clark 1995)

Mill, J.S., *On Liberty*, (first published 1859; many reprints, for instance in Everyman edition, London, Dent)

O'Donovan, O., *Resurrection and Moral Order*, (Leicester, IVP 1986)

Pierce, C.A., *Conscience in the New Testament*, (London, SCM 1955)

Pope John XXIII, *Pacem in Terris*, (London, CTS 1980)

Pope John Paul II, *Veritatis Splendor*, (London, CTS 1993)

Porter, J., *The Recovery of Virtue*, (London, SPCK 1990)

Ramsey, P., *Basic Christian Ethics*, (London, SCM 1953)

Ramsey, P., *Christian Ethics and the Sit-In*, (New York, Association Press 1961)

Ramsey, P., 'The Biblical Norm of Righteousness', *Interpretation* 24/4 (Oct 1970), pp. 419–29

Ramsey, P., 'The Case of the Curious Exception', in Outka, G.H., and Ramsey, P., *Norm and Context in Christian Ethics*, (London, SCM 1969)

Stafford, T., *Sexual Chaos*, (Leicester, IVP 1993)

Thatcher, A., *Liberating Sex*, (London, SPCK 1993)

Thielicke, H., *Theological Ethics 2: Politics*, (Grand Rapids, Eerdmans 1979)

Vasey, M., *Strangers and Friends*, (London, Hodder and Stoughton 1995)

Wilder, L.I., *By The Shores of Silver Lake*, (Harmondsworth, Puffin 1967, many reprints)

Index

abortion 18, 108, 189, 194
action and morals 105
Almond, Brenda 8
alternatives 15
Aquinas, Thomas 43, 173–177
arbitrary morality 18
Augustine 41
  virtues 42

Barth, Karl 43
behaviour, Christian 144
Bellah, Robert 7
Bible and ethics 155–169
biblical survey 64

casuistry 108
categories, moral 22
Channer, J.H. 195
children 84
Christian behaviour 144
  ethics 1, 32, 155–169
  love 32, 42, 44
  marriage 99
  moral witness 183–190
  tradition 95, 96
church discipline 148
code, moral 17
complexity, moral 22, 30
conflict 51–53
conscience 15, 170–182
conscientious objection 178
contraception 85

covenant and creation 72
  and kingdom 133
  and marriage 92
  and rules 100
  ethics 126
  love 35, 116
creation and covenant 72
  and death 114
  and kingdom 133
  and marriage 92
  and rules 100
  and sexuality 88
  doctrine 60
  ethics 62
  goodness 69
  motive 27
  order 68
  survey 64

death 114–116
discipline, church 148
  social 147
divorce 88, 90
  law 196
Dworkin, Ronald 127

ecology 191, 197
Ellul, Jacques 83
employment 76
ends and means 14
environment 81
environmental damage 191–193

ethics,
    Bible 155–169
    Christian 1, 32
    covenant 126
    creation 62
    value 126
euthanasia 101, 107, 114–128
everyday morality 7, 44

faithfulness 92
forgiveness 36, 112, 144–154
forgiving strangers 153

Giddens, Anthony 83
God's kingdom 133
    love 34
God's purpose 31, 98, 133
goodness of creation 69
guidance, Holy Spirit 55

Harvey, Anthony 88
Hauerwas, Stanley 87, 136–142
heart morality 55
Holy Spirit's guidance 55
homosexual marriage 97
homosexuality 88, 90

Illich, Ivan 83
illness and euthanasia 116–122
individualism 7
infanticide 108

Jesus' teaching 130, 151
Judaeo-Christian morals 26
justice 41, 148

kingdom fulfilment 133

language of values 9, 12, 16
law and morality 185
    and property 163
    enforcement 190
legalism 30, 108
legislation, environmental 191

liberalism 8
lies 47–51
life and death 114
    protection 116
literalist view 155
love 36–42
    and rules 46
    Christian 32, 42, 44
    covenant 35, 116
    God's 34
    motive 27
Luther 43

majority view 8
marriage 36, 84, 92
    Christian 99
    homosexual 97
McDonald, Ian 9
means and ends 14
Mill, J.S. 187
moral action 105
    categories 22
    code 17
    complexity 22, 30
    endeavour 146
    failure 24
    issues, new 25
    knowledge 140
    myths 8
    objectivity 27
    puzzle 3, 5
    reason 13
    rigour 1244–154
    rules 100–105
    simplicity 22, 30
    teaching 130
    thought 110
    values 9
    witness 183–190
moralism 30, 108
morality, arbitrary 18
    everyday 7, 8, 44
    heart 55
    Judaeo-Christian 26

roots 159
    social 18, 20
motives 24, 27
myths, moral 8

natural law 173
neutrality 8

O'Donovan, Oliver 140, 186–190
objective moral code 17, 27

parenthood 84
perfection, demand 130–142
permanent vegetative state 123
Pierce, C.A. 171
popular morality 55
pornography 188
preferences 15
premarital sex 97
property 78, 162
protection of life 116
punishment 148
purpose, God's 31, 98, 133
PVS 123

race discrimination 189
Ramsey, Paul 80, 94
reason, moral 13
relativism 8
responsibility 88
right and wrong 3
rules and love 46
    and morality 57
    application 51
    conflicting 51
    meaning 104
    moral 100–105

mythical 8

secular society 99
sex, premarital 97
sexuality 88
simplicity, moral 22, 30
social discipline 147
    morality 18, 20
suicide 107
Sunday trading 189, 197
superego 175

technology 81
terminal illness 116
Thatcher, Adrian 88
Thielicke, Helmut 192
toleration 8
tradition, Christian 95, 96
truth and speech 74
truth-telling 47–51, 100

unemployment 77
utilitarian arguments 161

value ethics 126
values 6–16
    language of 9, 12, 16
    weighing 14
Vasey, Michael 88, 98
views, moral 8
virtues, Augustine's 42

weighing of alternatives 15
    of values 14
Wilder, Laura Ingalls 79
witness, moral 183–190
work 76

The Meaning of Freedom
A Study of Secular, Muslim and Christian Views
J. Andrew Kirk

ISBN 0 85364 844 1

Recognising that increasingly Christians are seeing the need to understand and engage seriously with contemporary western culture, this book explores the concept of freedom in the west, its historical roots and current usage in diverse contexts.

The author considers the different meanings of freedom as held in western societies and assesses the strengths and weaknesses of each. He then examines Muslim views before setting out an alternative Christian vision which answers present dilemmas and contradictions.

J. Andrew Kirk has been Dean and Head of the School of Mission and World Christianity at Selly Oak Colleges, Birmingham since 1990. Amongst his previous publications are *God's Word for a Complex World* (Marshalls).

Pastoral Care and Counselling
A Manual
William K. Kay and Paul C. Weaver

ISBN 0 85364 784 4

A comprehensive, biblical guide for all those involved in pastoral ministry.

The first part of this book examines the call, lifestyle and responsibilities of a minister in the light of biblical teaching. The second deals with counselling of various kinds and in the context of bereavement, marital difficulties, unemployment and disruptive children. Personal difficulties such as low self-esteem are also covered.

Taken together, the two parts deal with pastoral care as a whole. The light they throw on the role of a minister will be helpful both to ministers and also to those who feel called to the pressures and problems of being a Christian today.

"A valuable and helpful resource which ought to be on every minister's and counsellor's book shelf." Selwyn Hughes

William Kay is Senior Research Fellow, Centre for Theology and Education. He writes from experience of pastoral life in Britain, preaching within Europe and from the prospective of academic research. He is co-author of *Drift from the Churches*.

Paul Weaver is the General Superintendent of British Assemblies of God and the pastor of New Life Church in Scunthorpe. He has been a full-time minister for more than twenty-five years.

Hated Without a Cause
A Survey of Anti-Semitism
Graham Keith

ISBN 0 85364 783 6

"If Christian churches are to repent of past attitudes and conduct towards the Jews, they need to be clear of what exactly they are to repent."

In this important book Graham Keith uses a dual approach to determine the nature of anti-Semitism in the Bible and in history, from Old Testament times to the contemporary Middle East situation. Examining the subject both theologically and historically, he supplies a realistic evaluation of the many influences that have contributed to the present situation and suggests how the church may react positively and sensitively.

Anti-Semitism in a live issue, both in Europe and in many Islamic countries. This survey supplies an excellent reference tool, with a substantial bibliography. It is also thought-provoking and will both inform and challenge all who read it.

"Every person with a concern for Jewish-Christian issues needs to read this book."
Martin Goldsmith, All Nations Christian College.

"A well-researched and lucidly written historical perspective . . . This is a very timely book, marked by sharp insight [and] generous sympathy."
David F. Wright, Senior Lecturer in Ecclesiastical History, University of Edinburgh.

". . . An immense contribution toward the understanding of anti-Semitism and the role that the Church has played, throughout the centuries."
David W. Torrance

Dr. Graham Keith teaches in Ayr. He has written a number of articles for the *Tyndale Bulletin*.